ALL OF GOD'S CHILDREN

Gene A. Nash

Order this book online at www.trafford.com
or email orders@trafford.com

Most Trafford titles are also available at major online book retailers.

Printed in the United States of America.

ISBN: 978-1-4669-9588-8 (sc)
ISBN: 978-1-4669-9589-5 (e)

Trafford rev. 10/08/2013

 www.trafford.com

North America & international
toll-free: 1 888 232 4444 (USA & Canada)
fax: 812 355 4082

Introduction

In every historical era there have been men who have had a profound effect on the lives of their contemporaries. There have been men who have been chosen by destiny to lead and inspire others to rise above the conditions in which life assigned them. Such a man in the nineteenth century was Abraham Jackson who was an illiterate slave. Abraham Jackson was born a slave in the Barnwell District of South Carolina, in 1837. He was a contemporary of Frederick Douglass. Douglass escaped from slavery at a young age and became a great abolitionist and spokesperson for the eradication of human bondage. Although he had the moral courage and demeanor of Frederic Douglass, Abraham was unable to successfully escape from slavery after several aborted attempts.

Many leading historians have written about the docile master-slave relationship point of view. This obedient—passive relationship was a myth on the plantation system of the South. Abraham Jackson defied this master slave connection through his numerous attempts to escape, although his venture was futile. However, through his resolve and resilience he accepted the harsh punishments at the hands of his slave-master. Because his desire and passion for freedom were greater than the slave system's willingness to break his will.

This book is about an ordinary man who lived in extra-ordinary times who lived during the period of slavery in Southern history. Abraham was born into an institution which viewed him as three-fifths of a white person by the United States Constitution. He was sold into the slave state of Georgia from South Carolina in 1856, one year before the infamous Dred Scott decision of 1857. This decision proclaimed in March of 1857, declared that African Americans were not citizens of the United States and could not sue in federal courts. A United States citizen had a constitutional right to take his slave property into any state or territory based on the property clause of the Fifth Amendment.

This book is not about the life of an invisible historical figure in a remote period of time in Southern and United Sates history. It's about a real person and his family who survived the brutality and savagery of slavery. This book is about a people who experienced disenfranchisement, the violence of the Ku Klux Klan, lynching, the loss of property through trickery, and deceit.

It's about a man who left his wife and four small children to join the union army. He wanted to be free. He arrived in Savannah on a cold rainy wind—swept day; dressed in raggedy clothes with worn out shoes with holes in each one. His body was exposed to the near freezing cold and rainy weather of March 1865. On March 7, 1865 he enlisted in the union army with Company C, Thirty-Third Regiment United States Colored Troops. Abraham knew that his fate and the future of thousands of other slaves depended upon the outcome of Union victory.

He learned to read and write while he was in the Union army. Slave law forbade him to learn to read and write. Under slave law in South Carolina and Georgia learning to read and write were forbidden. Severe punishment was inflicted on any slave who ventured to learn to read or write.

Abraham was mustered out of the Union army on January 31, 1866. Fort Wagner was located of Sullivan's Island near Charleston

South Carolina. Two and a half years earlier a bloody battle was fought between Union and Confederate forces at Fort Wagner. One of the first things he did upon his return to civilian life was to accept a five acre parcel of land from his former slave owner. This gave him and his family a new start; Abraham and his wife had four small children, two boys and two girls.

Nine years later he purchased a three-hundred acre tract of land in the summer of 1875. Later he built a school and church on part of his land in 1879 and 1892 respectively. Abraham and his two oldest sons, George and Lewis, and his friend Luke did most of the work in building the one-room school. His son-in-law was the first teacher in the one-room school. The school sat on a white sand hill surrounded by colorful wild flowers in spring. Israel's first class consisted of twenty five children and five were older African American adults. The older adults, according to their teacher, Mr. Israel Fraser wanted to learn to read the Bible. One of his students, a former slave declared "God hab brung us to de promised land," he proclaimed in his own dialect. "And us needs to learn de word of Gawd." In the 1890s according to undocumented oral history white children attended the school as well. White men attended the church called Beth Haven as late as the 1950s.

Gene A. Nash May 11, 2013

Chapter One

It was the spring of 1856 and the newly arrived slaves had been on their slave master's plantation less than four days. The trip to the new slave owner's plantation had taken six hours. Abraham knew that slaves were deprived of the rights held by free white men. Slaves were human chattel and could be bought and sold at the discretion of the slave owner. A rebellious or defiant slave would be severely punished, whipped, have fingers cut off, and on some plantations even a foot or hand amputated. This abusive punishment was a deterrent to other slaves who entertained any thought about escaping to freedom.

Abraham attempted to run away his fifth day on the Collins plantation. His ankles were still sore from the rough train ride from Savannah into the pine barrens of Tattnall County. A few minutes after daybreak Abraham made his move to escape. But he was betrayed by one of Massa Collins loyal slaves. "There he goes," Claude yelled out. Abraham dashed from the small slave cabin at full speed hobbled by sore ankles from the shackles around his ankles. "Get those dogs after him, and hurry up," shouted the overseer.

"Don't let him get far," yelled the large rotund man to the two slaves who were chasing Abraham through the woods west of "Massa Collins" farm as the other slaves called the place. The dogs trailed him about fifty yards behind. Abraham dashed across a small creek as the dogs increased their speed. A hundred yards from the creek Abraham slowed down and climbed up a tree. Minutes later, the dogs converged on the tree barking and jumping high into the air. The exhausted slaves chasing Abraham arrived four minutes later, wearied, and out of breath.

"Come down from there boy! We got you now, get on down," the obese overseer yelled.

"Call your dogs off, I'll come down. "Not before those dogs go." Master Collins arrived seconds later with his shotgun in one hand and his whip in the other. Abraham leaped from the tree falling on the dogs. He was chained and shackled and his first attempt to escape was unsuccessful. This was the first time he'd been chained and shackled. He was angry at himself for being taken captive.

An hour later, Abraham, the two faithful slaves, Master Collins and his overseer arrived back to the plantation. Both of Abraham's ankles were sore as they arrived at the big house and the area where unruly and disobedient slaves were punished. The obese overseer grabbed the whip from Master Collins. A delightful distasteful grin flashed across his face. "Jump to your feet, you black nigger, I'll teach you to run away from Mr. Collins place. You'll wish you never had feet when I finish with you."

The other slaves passively watched in a submissive manner as Abraham stood up to receive the sharp piercing lashes on his back. His hands were tied above his shoulders; his legs were spread apart to restrict his movement. The vile taskmaster turned and looked at the other slaves who stood trembling in fear. "What I'm going to do will teach the rest of you darkies a lesson. Never try to run away from Master Collins place. I'm going to tear the meat off his back with this whip."

The wicked overseer gave young Abraham twenty-five lashes across his back. The slave Claude held Abraham up as the overseer cut the rope from around his wrists and legs. Blood trickled slowly from his back as Claude carried him to the tiny slave cabin where

Abraham and four other slaves lived. That night Abraham was restless; the pain he suffered from the lashing was intolerable.

The next morning Master Collins had a young slave girl to attend to the whelps and scars on Abraham's back. The young slave girl was the granddaughter of mixed Cherokee Indian ancestry. She was of medium height with short hair and a pleasant friendly countenance. One of the female slaves said she saw Massa Collins wife cut off her hair after she saw him run his fingers through her hair in a rage of passion.

The pain from the rawhide whip was unbearable, as Abraham curled up in agony. The attractive slave girl was curious as she asked: "What's your name?"

"Who, that ain't your name now. Your name is Abraham Collins. Massa Collins will have big Claude to horsewhip you. Boy! You better forget that name Jackson."

"What's yo' name?" Abraham asked, in a sarcastic manner, as he rose from his cot.

"My name is Cinderella. Turn over here so I can rub this horse salve on your back. Don't talk. Let me clean that wound. Massa Collins will have you in the field at sunrise tomorrow."

"Ouch!" "That hurt, be careful, Abraham groaned."

"Cinderella is a pretty name," Abraham muttered. You ain't no princess, is you?"

"Remember: Your name is Abraham Collins. You is de property of Massa Collins."

Chapter Two

Two months later, Abraham was assigned the task of working with a slave twice his age. He was Joshua a slave who had been on the Collins' plantation for twenty years. The other slaves nicknamed Joshua "Sunrise" because he was always up each morning before sunrise. Abraham was assigned the task of working with the horses and mules along with Joshua. He was quick to learn that the horses were different from the mules as Sunrise often reminded him. The horses were different in size and strength as well as agility; they moved more swiftly than the mules. However, Abraham's goal was to escape to freedom whenever the opportunity arose.

Later that night Abraham got little sleep because the words of his father kept resonating in his mind. "Only your thoughts hold you captive as a slave, but your soul is free. You can look into the mind of your captor and see his weakness. The eyes of the buckra slave owners are evil and weak like the sparrow. Your eyes are as the eagle's sharp and full of wisdom. I can see God's mark upon you; no chains or shackles will be able to hold you. God has answered my prayer. I can see it in your eyes." Abraham remembered these words spoken by his father before he died. At his father's death Abraham was thirteen years of age. Abraham wondered if Joshua could be trusted. He enjoyed working with the horses and mules. Abraham was fascinated working with the horses and mules, but he wondered if Joshua could be trusted. He was a tall man who walked with a limp because a cask fell from a wagon and rolled over left leg. This happened in 1852. It didn't take ole Joshua long to learn that Abraham was different from the other captives on Master Collins' place. He'd already received twenty-five lashes for trying to escape during his first week on the Georgia plantation. One of Master Collins' loyal slaves revealed his plan of escape. Sunrise spoke to Abraham because he wanted to advise him:

"Now listen to me Abe, I knows dese white folks, dey will kill you if you don't do like dey tells you to do. You reminds me of some of dem colored folk dat my ole grand pappy talked 'bout, dey didn't wanna be captive and dey tried to 'scape. Dey ran away every chance dey gets. Some of dem niggers ran away down to Florida in the 1820s and 1830s. You knows dey joined dem Seminole Injuns. Some of dem niggers married into dere tribes; some of dem married Injun women. My ole grand pappy said some of dem became chiefs of de Seminole tribe. Two of dem niggers right here in Georgia kilt dere ole Massa up dere 'round Screven County; one chopped his ole Massa's head off wid an axe. My old grand pappy told me dis 'befo he died. Dey wuz from dat Africa; dey were members of dat Ibo tribe of dat country called Nigeria or sometin' like dat.

"Be careful what you say boy, 'yo job is to take care of dose hosses and mules. And any other task ole Massa Collins hab for you to do."

Abraham didn't know if he could trust Sunrise. If he was going to escape or think about running away, he was afraid to tell Sunrise. He would have to carefully choose the time; because the slaves on Massa Collins' place seemed to be content and satisfied with their fate. Abraham remained vigilant. He didn't want to arouse any suspicion when the time came for him to escape. He had heard of the failed attempts of Denmark Vessey and Nat Turner. He thought these slaves would've been successful if their fellow slaves hadn't betrayed them.

The next day after breakfast and before the signal was given for the slaves to work their assigned tasks; Abraham talked to the pretty young slave girl that had carefully consoled him and soothed the sores on his aching back. "Don't let ole Massa Collins find out you talk like you talk to me." Rilla warned Abraham.

"My name is Abraham Jackson, not Abraham Collins. I am not changing my name; I'm keeping the name of my first slave Massa."

"Don't let Massa Collins think that you is thinking 'bout learning to read or write either. He will give you another lashing and it will be harder than before. Be careful, and don't talk to him and the overseer likes you talk to me. Watch out for dat big Claude too, he can't be trusted. And never look those buckra straight in the eyes."

Abraham listened intently to what the pretty slave girl told him. The slave code of Georgia forbade slaves to learn to read and write. And slaves were forbidden to sue in the courts, testify against whites, buy and sell goods, enter into any type of contract. Slaves were the property of their owners and confined to the plantation or farm unless permitted by the owner to visit other plantations.

Before the weather became too hot, the slaves left to begin their daily work. Abraham gazed as if he was in a trance as the muscular black bodies unloaded the casks from the wagons. He was now a part of the gang that did the strenuous back breaking work. He remembered the blacksmith from Massa Miller's plantation who could bend iron with his bare hands The work of the male slaves were more strenuous than the female slaves. A few of the slaves were skilled at the tasks they performed.

Two women on Massa Collins place made all the cloth and clothes. They made everything that was needed on the plantation. Abraham was shocked to learn they did all the sewing on the Collins plantation and made beautiful clothes from the cloth that was given them or assigned for them to do. Abraham saw none of these things on Massa Miller's plantation in South Carolina. He carefully meditated on how he could escape from the forced labor on the Collins plantation and become a free man. He couldn't understand how the men and women were satisfied with their plight. The blacksmith, Abraham thought from his appearance appeared to be different from the others on the plantation. But could he be trusted, Abraham thought Claude had the same look, but betrayed him in his first attempt to escape to freedom.

Later that evening at dusk dark Abraham heard some of the slaves talk about Jesus. They were out of the sight of Massa Collins and his overseers, because they were careful not to let them hear or mention anything about religion or they would be severely punished. Abraham wanted to know what they were saying because no slaves could be caught in groups of more than three. He heard them talk about crossing the Jordan and the New Jerusalem; strange words to him. He heard Josh and Isaac talk about a land of milk and honey and that's where they'd be one day. "The good Lawd delivered Moses; he will deliver us chilun; the good Lawd delivered ole Daniel, He will deliver us too." They sang and gave praise to their God whom they thought would soon deliver them. They all marched back to their small cabins and turned in for the night.

The slaves knew the penalty if they were caught singing and praying, or talking about Jesus. The penalty was twenty-five lashes across their back. The leader of the group had two men to watch out for Massa Collins and his two overseers. If any of the slaves spotted Massa Collins or any of his men, they were to give two whistles in the sound of a whip-poor-will. The signal was for them to disperse back to their cabin.

Chapter Three

The slaves on the plantation worked six days per week, but were allowed to have fun, dance, and eat on Saturday afternoons for four hours. They were allowed to talk to each other and become more acquainted. There were twenty-one slaves on Massa Collins plantation including one mulatto. Abraham was watched closely by big Red, the nickname given to one of his two overseers and the trusted slave big Claude.

Charlie and Sunrise felt uncomfortable talking to Abraham because they didn't know what he would do or when he would do it. Charlie was over six feet tall, age twenty-nine, and had thick eyebrows and a missing middle finger on his left hand. Earlier Charlie informed Abraham of the special Saturday afternoons that were given to the slaves twice per month. Abraham was anxious to meet the pretty girl that came to his rescue and talk with her. But he felt the eyes of the wicked overseer watching his every move. He walked the Small enclosed area looking for Cinderella but didn't see her. He began to think about where she could be and what she was doing. Soon the frolic was over and Abraham was unable to see her.

Early the next morning before the slaves left for their assigned task Abraham questioned Sunrise. He wanted to know if Sunrise knew Cinderella. He asked him all kinds of questions. "When did you last see her? "What was she talking about? Did she seem happy?

"When did I see who? I doesn't know who you is talking 'bout. Pull yoself together."

"The pretty girl that worked on my back, you know her." Abraham declared with a smile on his face. "What happened to her Sunrise?"

"I heard she mixed wid Injun; you don't want to bother with her boy."

"I is gwine to see her today," Abraham muttered.

"Here he comes, ole Massa Collins," Sunrise said sheepishly.

The slaves knew something was wrong when the slave boss came around that early. But he stopped halfway; turned around and went back toward the barn waving his right hand for John and Claude. Sunrise was happy to see Massa Collins move in a different direction.

"Who is she Sunrise? What is her name?" Abraham growled.

"Cinderella, but She calls herself Rilla."

"Cin who; I can't say that name. Pretty girl, I is going to give her that name.

Sunrise, just call her pretty girl. She fixed up my back, she saved my bones," Abraham Smiled.

Abraham and Sunrise immediately sensed something was wrong. Massa Collins decided to come back. The last time he came around that early was when Abraham and three other slaves were brought in from South Carolina. And two slaves were caught that had run away from the Brewton Farm. They were recaptured and returned to their owner. A rumor circulated on the plantation that some of the slaves were engaged in religious activities. Massa Collins talked to them before they went to their assigned tasks.

"I want all of you to know," he muttered, slapping a black leather strap into his left hand. "There will be no preaching and praying around here. If you want to pray, tell me and I will pray to God for you." Massa Collins' reprimand of them fell on deaf ears. Abraham observed the ways of the older slaves on the plantation and agreed with them. They were careful not to let anyone find out where they met or the time.

It was rumored by Sallie and Alice that one large slave owner in the county allowed his slaves to attend the church of their choice in the little community ten miles from Massa Collins plantation. His slaves attended church every Sunday as a part of their routine. In South Carolina, Massa Miller allowed his slaves to attend church one Sunday out of each month. And the other Sundays they were free to visit each other. Two weeks earlier, Abraham divulged this to Sunrise and Charlie before his first secret meeting with the other slaves that met in seclusion.

Abraham had heard about free African Americans and their religious activities in the county. It was a violation of the law for free African Americans in the town of Reidsville and the adjoining counties to worship freely with whites. He and the other slaves knew that free African Americans lived in Tattnall County. The census of 1850 listed a considerable number of free blacks in the county. Their lives were much better than their slave counterparts; a few free African Americans were owners of farms in the county and had property values higher than some whites. Ninety percent of the free blacks in the county were mulattoes. The slaves often referred to mulattos as "high yellows," because of their highly visible light complexion. Sunrise and Charlie jokingly alluded to them by that hilarious epithet.

Chapter Four

In October at the end of the harvest season, the male slaves' major task was digging up stumps and cutting down trees. Later they would build rafts and float the logs down the Ohoopee and Altamaha Rivers to the city of Darien, Georgia. Rafting timber down the river required strong bodies to stir the raft in the right direction. It sometimes took six hours or more to get the timber to the landing to be floated downstream. Abraham, Sunrise, Charlie, and Henry arrived at daybreak to begin the difficult task of moving and rafting timber. The journey from the Ohoopee downstream into the Altamaha was an all day venture. Rafting timber was one of the most exhaustive and dangerous work tasks performed by slaves. Black bodies could be seen on the river for miles guiding the rafts that carried the logs to the timber market. The presence of danger was always invariably on the minds of the slaves and Massa Collins. The danger of hitting a sandbar or large rock was always present.

Abraham thought this could be his opportunity to escape to freedom. But he was mindful that he had to overcome Red and big Claude who always rode the timber rafts to ensure a trip without strife or rebellion. Abraham thought it would be easier if something went wrong; he could escape in the deep water and swim his way to freedom. He wanted to get away without being captured. If captured and returned to bondage his opportunity to escape to freedom may never come again. He knew traveling in the swamps would be difficult. He'd heard of the large swamp to the south with an Indian name; but he couldn't pronounce it. The Indians called it the Okefenokee Swamp close to sixty miles from the Ohoopee River. He didn't want to get caught in that area. He could be attacked by ferocious animals and never reach the Florida border to the south that Sunrise talked about.

A few miles downstream the raft carrying Abraham and Charlie slammed into a large rock, whirled around and hit a sandbar which was invisible to them. A second raft slammed into the first one carrying Henry, big Claude, and Sunrise. The impact from the collision caused the logs to rip apart. They began to move quickly in the swift and swollen current. All of the men were thrown backward into the dark waters of the Ohoopee.

"Get those logs back together, hurry it up you darkies! We ain't got no time to waste," Red shouted. "We don't want dark to catch us playing in the water!" Get to moving Claude you and Abraham."

"Yessuh boss, we is moving, we is gwine to git 'em" big Claude yelled out.

"Get them logs," Red growled in anger. He never lost his rifle; he had it in his right hand as he rested against a rock. "I will shoot any nigger that tries to escape." Red yelled. Many logs had come to a standstill in the swift moving water. "Hurry up! Move faster and get those damn logs together." Darkness will catch us out here in the water. For every log we lose, that'll be ten lashes across your back." The mean overseer shouted.

Abraham looked quickly to see if he could see Josh or Charlie. He checked to see if they were injured. He saw neither one, and glanced to see if Henry was in his view. He didn't see Henry and wondered if he was in any danger. A heavy rain fell for three days the previous week. The torrential rains caused the water to rise rapidly. Immediately Abraham spotted Charlie and Sunrise, but didn't see Henry.

"Boss, I don't see Henry," Abraham yelled out, as the water roared and splashed against the logs and the trapped debris.

"Get those logs tied together, Henry is around somewhere. Keep moving we'll find Henry somewhere. Where is that big nigger Claude, "Red screamed out to Abraham and Charlie. "Don't anyone try to run away. You'll get a bullet if you do. Get those logs back together." The swiftly moving water began to dissipate as Abraham and Charlie spotted Henry. But Claude was missing.

"Boss: I sees Henry." Abraham's voice was barely audible.

"Where is he?" Red looked around to see if anyone was trying to escape in the swollen current. "Over here boss, by this tree," Abraham pointed in the direction of the jammed logs. He threw his right hand in the air then swam in the direction of Henry. Henry's left foot was entangled in a root, close to sixty feet away from Abraham.

"Over here Abraham, Hurry! I'se can't move; my foots is caught." Here was Abraham's chance to escape to freedom. Chaos and confusion were all around him, he had to think quickly. Would he try to swim his way across the river to freedom or would he help Henry. He thought for a split second, if he helped to free Henry the four of them could overpower Red and big Claude. Another obstacle penetrated his thoughts; the river was full of other travelers on their way to the lumber market. He faced another dilemma, could he trust Henry or Charlie? He never believed that he could trust Sunrise. Sunrise seemed happy being Massa Collins slave. But now maybe all of them could escape. Abraham Spotted Red and Claude move in the direction toward Charlie and Sunrise. Red began cussing: "Massa Collins is going to sell all of you away.

"Get them damn logs together, it'll be dark after while." He continued to yell out. Abraham saw a snake moving in the direction of Henry. He was the first to see the viper. He grabbed a large stick floating past him and snatched it from the water. The snake moved closer toward Henry. "Hurry Abraham, come on!" Henry cried out. Abraham slammed the large stick against the snake's head as he rushed to untangle Henry's feet from the root. With one blow he whacked the snake's head off; Henry began praising the Lord as he was disentangled from the root.

The farther downstream the raft traveled the swift flowing current began to diminish. Two white tail deer were seen running and jumping near the edge the river. The slave crew and Red saw a large catamount chase after one of the deer. There were stories in the county that all types of wild animals were seen on the Ohoopee and the Altamaha. Abraham contemplated, if he didn't make his move now; would there be another opportunity? He began to investigate the consequences for and against his chances of escaping to freedom. The river was full of overseer's and paddy rollers, but they were from other farms and plantations. Maybe he could make it to the swamp and follow a path to the South. He could travel during the darkness of night and hide out during the day. But he didn't want to travel through that giant swamp with the Indian name. At his young age he'd heard so many dangerous tales about the Okefenokee with its mire and quicksand. He'd heard Sunrise tell tales about human cannibals eating babies and other human beings.

Two hours later they were still swimming in the water chasing logs and repairing and patching up the rafts. Abraham surmised they could spend the remainder of the day in the chilly November water. The thought of escaping still meandered through his mind; what if he escaped and was captured. He could be sold to another plantation or farm; whom could he trust, would Joshua or Charlie betray him; he had to do something. He could make his move now or endure the pain of remaining the property of Massa Collins.

It was approaching dark. Red, Claude, Abraham and the other slave made camp fifty yards inland from the river. The rotund overseer decided they had to work faster the next day and make an early start. At daybreak they began to get the equipment that was needed to move downstream and into the Altamaha. Abraham's chance of escaping to freedom was delayed. He felt the obstacles were too overwhelming against his escaping. The sparkling sunlight began to peep from behind the tree tops as daylight shone upon the Ohoopee.

Abraham began to think about what he heard Massa Collins saying to the slave owners at the slave sale in Savannah. He heard them laughing and talking about how happy the slaves were on his plantation in Georgia. He told Massa Miller his slaves loved to sing, laugh, and dance. This type of behavior was good for slave morale on his place, he cautioned Massa Miller. He made known to him that his slaves were seldom sick. He also noted that his female slaves were good breeders and good at sewing and making clothes. He specified that all of the slaves' clothes were made right there on his place by two slave women. Abraham stood and listened amid the cries and screams of those who protested vehemently against being sold away.

"No nigger ever tries to run away from my place. My boys and bloodhounds would grab him before he got within fifty yards of his escape". Massa Collins laughed."

Abraham thought about what Massa Collins had said. He never mentioned Massa Collins conversation to anyone else. He kept this matter to himself. He saw none of the happy, laughing, or dancing slaves that Massa Collins indicated. He felt that one day he would make a successful escape to freedom. To keep another human being in bondage wasn't God's law and was no laughing matter. He felt that one day slave owners would have to pay for their crimes against humanity. He listened to Massa Collins talk about how the nation was divided over the slavery issue. The North was trying to interfere with their way of life. He heard him talk with other slave owners about how the South provided the rest of the nation with agricultural products and exports to England and France.

Chapter Five

A year had passed since the dangerous encounter on the Ohoopee River in which Abraham had almost lost his life swimming in the swift current to retrieve the runaway logs and rebuilding the timber rafts. At this point he was happy because he had almost achieved one of his two goals; his first goal was to escape to freedom; and his second goal was to marry the pretty young slave girl. However, his first encounter nearly cost him his life. He escaped early one morning about three hours before dawn amidst heavy intermittent rain showers. He had his escape route well planned. His number one goal was to escape southward into Florida. He had heard Sunrise tell many stories about how runaway slaves found safe haven in Florida among the Seminole Indians decades earlier, and how the Seminoles accepted them as equals. But all young Abraham wanted to do was receive his freedom. He entertained unpleasant thoughts wondering if he would see his mother and brothers again. It had been five years since he last saw them. They could be sold away to another plantation or even killed by a depraved slave owner. It was almost daybreak. He had traveled nearly five miles without seeing any human being. He'd only heard the sound of an owl or an occasional bird swoop down in front of him scaring him half senseless.

As the hours passed he grew more nervous and cautious not knowing when he would encounter slave catchers looking for runaways of which he was one. He grew hungry and thirsty, but kept moving through the thick vegetation. Suddenly he spotted two men on horseback riding in his direction, the horses moved in a slow trot. A third man on horseback moved at a slower pace trailing about one hundred feet behind the two men. He kept a close watch on the third man as he approached him. The two men stopped and waited for the third man. The three looked sharply in the direction where Abraham was hiding. He looked to see if he recognized any of the riders. Suddenly the three men rode off and when they were out of sight he cautiously crossed the road to the other side. He believed that he was around twenty miles from the Collins plantation. He was famished and had grown weak from a lack of food. To his right he stepped down into a muddy water hole and spotted a large fish. He placed his right hand in the water, grabbed the slippery fish and fell to the ground as the fish slipped out of his hand. He broke off a piece of limb and jabbed it through the fish's head. Minutes later he had his first food in nearly twelve hours. He followed the winding creek for another mile; then walked upon a persimmon tree. The large overripe berry was a faded orange in color. He reached up the tree and grabbed four and began to eat with the stems on them.

The next morning he was awaken by two men with a rifle poked in his ribs. He had fallen asleep in his quest to escape to freedom; he knew that his chance of escaping to freedom was over. He slowly opened his eyes, things were blurry at first. But he recognized one of the men. He had seen him at the lumber mill in Darien along with three other men and five slaves. The man was tall and thin with a red mustache and two missing front teeth. "Hey nigger: Wake up. What are you doing here? Whose nigger are you? What's your name?" He shouted to Abraham. He poked him in the ribs with the rifle as the other man looked on. What's your name?" The fast talking man didn't give Abraham a chance to answer. Suddenly, he answered.

"I don't know." He mumbled looking off in another direction. A man rode by in a wagon and happened to look over and see what was happening. He stopped and climbed down from his wagon. The two men greeted each other and said to the man with the red mustache "I know this little nigger; he belongs to that Collins man. He escaped two days ago. My name is Jim Ford."

"I am James Smith and this is Henry Brewton."

"What's your name nigger? He asked Abraham?

"I don't know, Abraham grinned. "But I show can sing and I can dance. If you gives me some food and water."

"Nigger, are you trying to be funny. Get up, stand on your feet. We're going to put chains and shackles on you. Mr. Collins got twenty slaves and you're the only one who tried to run away. When I finish with you, you won't try it again. Mr. Collins will have your feet chopped off. Then you won't be able to run. Now what's your name?

"I don't know. I can't remember, Abraham again said. Boss, I can't read and I can't write. The law says I is de property of Massa Collins. But, I can sing and I can dance."

"What's your name nigger? Boys this is a funny nigger, but I ain't laughing."

Abraham continued to trick them. "My name is Nat Turner."

The next morning the two men brought Abraham back to the Collins plantation. He walked chained and shackled behind the man who spotted him lying in the tall grass. His dream of escaping to freedom had turned into a nightmare. Abraham had traveled about five miles from the Collins plantation before he succumbed to hunger and fatigue. The slow trek back was a painful journey. The chains and shackles had bruised his ankles and the lower part of his legs just above his ankles. The two men on horseback steered him back to the Collins plantation with the sound of the bull whip popping in his ears. They arrived on the plantation about an hour before dawn. Roosters were crowing and dogs were heard barking a mile away as the sound carried in the still of morning. Slave men and women prepared to go to the field to begin their days work.

An hour later rabbits were seen near the edge of the slave quarters as they scurried into the woods hopping and leaping as two dogs chased after them. The slaves were ready to begin their day's task. Fear ran rapidly in the small slave quarters in the early morning hour. They knew what happened to a slave whose attempt to escape was unsuccessful. This was Abraham's second futile attempt to escape to freedom. He knew he would be openly flogged where all the slave men and women and small children would see him. This lashing would discourage any other slave who entertained thoughts of escaping from Massa Collins place. Abraham's back was barely healed from his first horse whipping. He was given thirty-five lashes across his back until his skin was broken and the blood began to trickle down.

"This will teach him a lesson boss," the overseer drew back his whip. "He won't try and run away anymore, he knows his place now." The overseer spoke in a loud voice staring at Sunrise, Charlie, and the others, a taunting smile flashed across Big Claude's face.

The slaves and the mean scar-faced overseer remembered what had happened two years earlier when Abraham failed to recognize Collins as his last name. The slaves were shocked that Abraham received only thirty-five lashes. The cruel overseer began to taunt Abraham as he asked him his name again: "What's your name nigger?" Abraham was buried in pain and could hardly hear what was being asked. The intrepid slave whispered "Abraham Jackson," falling over on his face.

"You fool! Tell him your name is Abraham Collins," the young slave woman ran toward Abraham. "Don't say dat anymore," she protested.

"Get out of the way you wench," the overseer hollered as he knocked her to the ground. "Boss! They all need to be taught a lesson." Red screamed! Abraham slowly pulled himself to his feet; he started to move, but fell backward and then to his knees. The intolerable pain flashed across his face as he grimaced and propelled himself forward. He heard the voice of a man speaking in what appeared to be a whisper. "That'll teach him and all the other niggers a lesson. They can't run away from here."

An hour later Abraham sat on the side of his crude bed. The young slave woman that had taken care of him when he was severely beaten once before, again, attended to his wounds. Rilla's mother, Milly, warned young Abraham to accept the name of his Massa and accept his fate as a slave. He was annoyed and infuriated with himself for being unable to escape to freedom. The next day he experienced severe pain, but went quietly to work at his task in the field and spoke not a word to Sunrise or Charlie. They understood his dilemma and were sympathetic with his predicament. Unable to carry on his task, Abraham soon collapsed to his knees. Charlie and Sunrise became frighten as to what action to take. They grabbed Abraham and carried him back to the cabin. Then they hurried back to their assigned tasks.

Later that night, the pain had subsided. Rilla worked on his back while he was asleep and in a semi-conscious state of mind. Abraham awakened from sleep and began carefully to reflect on his life as a slave on the Miller plantation in South Carolina. He meditated about when he was a young boy of no more than ten years of age. The last whipping he received in Carolina was unspeakable for a eleven year old; it left a visible scar on his left shoulder for close to two years. He received a lashing for turning over a bucket of water. This accident enraged the overseer and Abraham received ten lashes for his obstinate behavior. He was angered because of what happened to his father and he wanted to lash out in a vindictive manner.

Before he returned to sleep he began to think of more pleasant thoughts. He smiled within his soul every time he thought of

Rilla and how she attended to his wounds after he was whipped after each fruitless attempt to escape. He began to think, some of the things she said to him made sense. Maybe he shouldn't have a confrontation with Massa Collins about his name. He was no longer a slave of Joe Jackson who treated him with more consideration. He felt that Massa Jackson knew that he was slave property, but at the same time felt that slaves were human beings. Massa Miller nor Massa Collins shared this thought.

Abraham heard the echo of her words in his mind: "You wants to run away every chance you gets. Massa Collins will cut-off your foots one of dese days. You'll be a cripple then. He may sell you away from here; they can do worse things to a young black man. You doesn't want dat to happen."

Three hours later it was daybreak and time for Abraham, Sunrise, and Charlie to begin work at their daily task. They fed the horses and mules, gave them water and were ready to begin work. They worked all morning planting the spring crop with thirty minutes for lunch.

Abraham received little sleep because of the pain in his back and the sores that were there as a result of the whipping. He was awakened by the words of what Rilla had spoken to him earlier. He knew that one day slavery would come to an end and he'd be a free man. When would the day come was the question that bombarded his thinking. He had heard Massa Collins talk to other slave owners about the status of slavery. He heard them talk about the recent Supreme Court decision in the Dred Scot case and how it affected slavery in the South. The abolitionists were fighting to bring an end to slavery. The newly elected president, James Buchannan was a proslavery person in the white house. Harriet Beecher Stowe's book Uncle Tom's Cabin was a blow to the slaveholders cause. The book was a good fortune to the Northern abolitionists and a sour apple and an omen to the south. The sale of this book President Abraham Lincoln sarcastically stated helped cause the Civil War.

It was near the end of the work day for the slaves. Abraham, Charlie, and Sunrise had just come in from the field. They planted corn all day and were now attending to the horses and mules. Abraham was exhausted from the grueling day's work. He had little sleep the night before. The workday of a slave began at daybreak and was over when the sun went down in late afternoon. The slaves had the privilege to engage in any activity they wished after a day's work; as long as they complied with Massa Collins rules. They couldn't leave the plantation without an approved pass. No more than four slaves could congregate together in a group. They couldn't look the slave owner or any white person in his or her eyes. Abraham didn't like any of these rules. He said within himself-I must not let the buckra man know that I am in pain.

The slave cabins on the Collins plantation were small crude buildings. They all had dirt floors, a small table on each side of the room and two small beds in each cabin. Abraham didn't like the odor that emanated from the dirt floor, but soon grew accustomed to it. Each day the small buildings appeared to Abraham to grow smaller. Each slave cabin had a wood frame door about five foot and ten inches tall.

Chapter Six

The last day of April arrived on the Collins plantation and Abraham was thinking of proposing marriage to Rilla. He thought that Massa Collins was a vindictive man and would forbid his marriage to Rilla. Because of his attempts to run away, although unsuccessful he would certainly prevent his marriage to Rilla. Massa Collins would control his marriage because his wife would still be Massa Collins property. The children born of the marriage would be the property of ole Massa Collins. He thought of being sold to another slave owner or being sold into the middle part of the state or even out of the state.

He believed that Massa Collins was fond of Rilla. She was the one who attended to his wounds each time he was brutally whipped. He hadn't seen Massa Collins whip her or instruct his overseer to lash her. He took a liking to Milly as well. She had been a slave on the Collins plantation since 1839, close to twenty years. Abraham was twenty-one and Rilla was sixteen. He thought that Rilla was older than sixteen because of the way she carried herself. He heard Sunrise tell Charlie that she was three years older than what Abraham thought. Rilla had two brothers Frank, ten and Henry eight.

The next day was the first day of May and Abraham finally mustered the courage to ask Rilla to marry him. He left his cabin and strolled down to where she and her mother were. He was going to ask her two weeks ago, but became uneasy and couldn't find the right words. He finally arrived and knocked on the door. No one came to open the door and nearly twenty seconds later Milly opened the door. "Hello Miss Milly, how is you dis morning?" Abraham politely asked. "Jest common, "Milly commented. Abraham thought he smelled food cooking, but he knew better. Slaves didn't have what he scented. He looked around the small cabin, but didn't see Rilla.

Rilla walked in from the outside, Abraham turned around and saw her. Surprised to see her, he almost fainted. "How is you dis morning?" "Rilla, I have sometin' to ask you. "I ain't seed her lately." She was curious to know what Abraham wanted to ask. They were all still standing since Rilla was the last to walk in. "We all best sit down," Milly said. In the cabin were one large wooden chair and one small chair. Abraham sat in the larger chair. He was already anxious and excited.

"Take for betta or worse," you mean. He thought to himself.

"Yes, I wants to marry you. I's been meaning to ask you for two weeks." Abraham's voice firm and steady; his uneasiness seemed to have left. Milly looked at both Abraham and Rilla while they were talking. Rilla was sixteen and seemed a rather mature young woman. She was beautiful with long black hair which had grown in length since Massa Collins wife cut it in a rage of anger. Abraham kept waiting for an answer. He didn't want to ignite his fears of Massa Collins not wanting him to marry her.

"Boy has you stop trying to run away? 'Cause, you doesn't hab anywhere to go, Milly growled. Well I ain't heard anything else 'bout you trying to 'scape. What does you say Rilla 'bout marrying him."

"Yes, I will mama." Rilla said with excitement in her voice. Abraham was ecstatic to hear that. His fear of asking was now over. He wanted to be married by a preacher. He desired a small simple wedding. The traditional slave marriage consisted of jumping over a broom. He strongly disliked this type of ceremony. He'd known and heard of slave marriages being performed by preachers on other farms and plantations. He'd even heard of the slave master performing marriage ceremonies.

The following Saturday afternoon Abraham and Rilla were married, not by a preacher but by Massa Collins. Abraham was disappointed that he and Rilla didn't have the pleasure of a preacher performing their marriage. He made peace within his soul and grew satisfied with the arrangement. He knew that one day the slaves would be free and then he and Rilla would be able to have a legal marriage ceremony. He'd heard of free blacks in the county that had their marriage in churches, and that's what he wanted for him and Rilla.

All of his friends wished him and Rilla well. Sunrise and Charlie were happy for him and Rilla. He even heard that Massa Collins agreed with their marriage. All the slaves had a frolic that evening something they got to do on occasions such as this and at Christmas and whenever Massa Collins arranged for them to have one. Rilla agreed with Abraham that she should move in his small cabin with him. All the buildings in the slave quarters were approximately the same size. Abraham was glad for Rilla that she and her mother lived on the same plantation. Her two brothers, Frank and Henry lived there as well. Abraham knew more about Rilla and her family than she knew about him. He knew nothing about her father because she or Milly seldom mentioned his name.

In their small cabin two kerosene lamps were the source of light for them. Two candles burned on each side of the room on their wedding night. Abraham had known Rilla was the woman he'd marry time he laid eyes on her. He was attracted to her when she volunteered to nurse his wounds each time Massa Collins' overseer horse-whipped him. He believed she was a good cook, but had only eaten food she'd brought him one time. He thought most young women Rila's age were good cooks. He reminded himself daily that he was married but Massa Collins controlled his every move. He enjoyed her singing. She had a scintillating voice as Abraham soon discovered. He wondered how she was able to sing songs and hymns and couldn't read or write. All slaves on the plantation were illiterate, but some had talent for singing. Her singing was pleasing to his ears. He was told that her mother Milly could sing, but he'd never heard her.

Abraham would never read the works of Shakespeare, Browning, Phyllis Wheatley, or other famous people in the field of poetry or prose. He had heard of the famous northern abolitionist William Lloyd Garrison and Frederick Douglass; but he'd never heard them speak. Slavery denied him the right to learn to read and write. Slave states passed codes which forbade slaves to learn to read or write. Abraham's mind continued to be bombarded with thoughts and questions about slavery and humanity. Did the slave owners feel any humanity in their hearts for their slaves? How could slaves who were made in the image of God be classified as human chattel? As long as he was a slave his mind would be held captive. He would be unable to think and explore ideas as a free person could.

During the first six months of their marriage he and Rilla grew closer to each other. They grew closer as the days passed. He and Rilla still were distressed over the thought of being separated by sale. Any slave young or old could be sold at the slave owner's discretion. Rilla hadn't ever been sold, but Massa Collins' was Abraham's third slave owner. Slavery had been an institution in Georgia since 1752. From its founding in 1733 slavery was forbidden by the state's charter. The argument for its prohibition was that the state was founded upon humanitarian purposes; to free imprisoned debtors who'd crammed the penal institutions of England.

George, Abraham and Rillas' first child was born on January 5, 1859. Another memorable event occurred in December of

1859. John Brown was hanged for attacking the federal arsenal at Harper's Ferry in Virginia. Brown had hoped to free the slaves there and start a slave uprising in the slave states.

Abraham and the slaves on Massa Collins' plantation looked forward to the day when they would throw off their chains and shackles. The majority of the slaves on Massa Collins' plantation knew little or nothing about Georgia or Tattnall County. Most of them had heard of the Altamaha and Ohoopee Rivers. The slave owners kept their human chattel away from books and any learning materials. A slave would be severely punished with the whip if caught trying to learn to read and write.

Sunrise was different from other slaves on the plantation. He kept his ears attuned to what was being said without being suspect. He listened for every word that was spoken about freedom, slave sales, and every conversation that would help the slave's cause. He told Abraham and Charlie that he learned from his pappy and grand pappy. They told him a lot of things before his grand pappy died and his pappy was sold. "Keep your ears open boys, and listen to what the buckra man is saying. We can't read or write, but the buckra will say tings dat'll keep you alive. Don't let 'em see you looking at him. Remember, you can learn wid'yo' ears if you keeps em'open."

Sunrise heard Massa Collins and Massa Tippins engaged in a conversation one morning. They talked about Milledgeville, Augusta, and Louisville. Sunrise couldn't pronounce the names of these three cities. He had no idea that Augusta and Louisville had been capitals of Georgia and Milledgeville was its present capital. He heard them say that Savannah was Georgia's oldest city and first capital, why they mentioned that he didn't know.

An hour later Sunrise continued talking: "Yesditty, I seed Massa Collins wid a newspaper in his hand. Ole Massa didn't see me but I seed him. I was taking some tings out de wagon for him. Dey was talkin' 'bout some niggers in dat county of Liberty. Dey said dat dey is a lot of niggers in dat county. Ole Massa was reading from dere county newspaper de Hinesville Gazette. He was telling Massa Tippins dat five slaves ran away from dere ole Massa."

"Last Sunday, I hears, ole Massa Collins and Massa Eason talk 'bout niggers in dem counties MCIntosh and Liberty. Dey said de slaves out number de buckra. Ole Massa Eason tells Massa Collins dey have as many niggers as white people."

"Ole Massa Collins and de slave bosses in dis county is 'fraid. Dey don't know what is gwine to happen. Abraham snickered.

"Massa Collins 'don hab nuttin' to worry 'bout. Ain't dat many niggers in dis county. Dey is all in Liberty and McIntosh counties. Us slaves here is 'fraid of de bullwhip and de cowhide. We ain't going anywhere. We lubes ole Massa Collins, Sunrise roared in laughter"

"Well boys, I'se gwine to see my wife and baby," Abraham chuckled.

The next morning Abraham started his work task shortly after he left his cabin. He and Sunrise gathered the horses and mules and prepared them for the day's task. Sunrise as usual lived up to his nickname. He was up earlier than anyone else and was ready to begin his task. He heard that Massa Collins was ready to issue their summer and winter clothes. Slave owners had told their slaves not to think about what they would wear. The Master would provide for them just like the good Lord provide food and raiment for them. Clothing would be issued to them after they finished work for the day.

For days there was talk out of Milledgeville that Georgia would secede from the Union if Abraham Lincoln was elected President in the Fall. The Slave and Free States were still divided over the Dred Scott decision. Both political parties were divided over the extension of slavery into the Free states. The High Court had already ruled that the Missouri Compromise was unconstitutional.

Southern Democrats including Senator Alexander Stephenson of Georgia applauded the ruling.

Arguments continued over the Fugitive Slave Act. Southerners wanted the Act upheld and reinforced. The law gave everyone the right to chase down escaped slaves. Northern abolitionists strongly opposed this law. Under the Fugitive Slave Law free blacks could be tracked down and sold into slavery. The institution of slavery was driving the North and the South further and further apart. Runaway slaves always faced the danger of being captured and returned to bondage. The Fugitive Slave law was passed seven years before Abraham was sold from South Carolina into Georgia. This law was part of a constitutional process that forced authorities in the free states where slavery was forbidden to return fugitive slaves to their rightful owner.

Later that evening after the work day ended the overseer and Massa Collins came by and issued everyone new clothes for summer and winter. Abraham and Sunrise received the clothes for their group and Milly and Rilla received clothes and provisions for the female slaves.

The male slaves received one suit for the entire year. There was no provision for variation in seasonal temperature. They received one hat, a pair of shoes, and two cotton shirts; one for summer and one for winter. All the slaves enjoyed receiving additional clothing.

The next day shortly after breakfast Abraham had a question for Charlie: "Massa Collins talks 'bout a perfect world when Jesus comes. Why can't we hab one now, Charlie?"

"I don't know Abraham."

"All dis crazy talk 'bout Dred Scott decision, 'cesion and run-away slave law I don't know what dey is talking 'bout. Let de ole slave bosses kill each udder. I hear dey talking 'bout states' rights." From what I hears, its 'bout us po slaves, Abraham mumbled.

"Gawd is gwine to fight our battles. He's gwine to knock dese hoes right out of our hands. Henry guffawed. Dey should've 'lef our grand mammies and grand pappies in Africa" Charlie growled.

"Where is ole Sunrise?" Abraham asked looking toward the barn. "It's time to work. Maybe old Sunrise is tinking 'bout running away to his freedom. Maybe he is gwine back to old viginny."

Chapter Seven

Eight months later on March 4, 1860 Abraham and Rilla's second child was born. It was a girl and they named her Harriet. Once again Abraham and Rilla were proud parents of a baby girl. The baby was delivered by the midwife who had delivered their first child in January 1859. Abraham lifted the fragile new-born into his hands and mumbled "dis baby won't be Massa Collins servant. She's gwine to be a free person. Just like de birds and de butterflies." Abraham beamed with approval.

"I wants dem to learn to read and write. I wants dem, Abraham to hab an eddication."

Rilla was a proud mother. She and Abraham had two children, a boy and a girl. Their happiness and hope could easily turn to despair. The thought of a child being separated from his parents by sale was a continuous fear of both Abraham and Rilla. "I pray to de Lawd, dat we'll neber be separated," Rilla peered.

"I seed dat ole so called African magic man yesditty. He wuz looking for you," Milly said looking at Abraham.

"What do dat ole African wants wid me?" Abraham frowned.

"He says he's got sometin' to give you. He says he's gwine to wait 'til it gits dark, den he's gwine to come 'round." Milly snarled. "I seed ole Miss Sarah yesditty afternoon. She and ole Massa dey is 'scarid."

For the past two days Master Collins was seen in the fields talking and intermingling with the slaves. Sunrise and Henry thought this was a little strange. Isaac considered his behavior weird. Massa was rarely seen in the fields among the slaves. He had his overseer and two of his loyal slaves to carry out his schemes. He looked awkward in the fields with his slaves.

"Lawd, sometin' is wrong wid ole Massa. He hardly leaves de big house," Isaac said to Sunrise.

"How are you doing today, Isaac?" Massa Collins grinned as he spoke to Isaac. Isaac was utterly shocked.

"I'se fine Massa suh," Isaac mumbled with his head down staring at the ground. What hab happened to ole Massa, Isaac mumbled to himself. "I'se trying to finish dis work Massa, suh."

The slaves were shocked at the attention received from their slave boss. This was the first time they'd seen him behave in this manner. Abraham, Sunrise, and Charlie were crafty, they saw Massa Collins, but he didn't see them. They knew that things were going bad for the South. There was talk of the Southern states seceding from the Union. The Republican Party and the abolitionist wanted to abolish slavery. They wanted the Fugitive Slave Act abolished. The Southern Democrats wanted slavery extended into the territories received from the Mexican War.

There had been talk of a slave uprising in the South and in Georgia. John Brown's attack on the federal arsenal at Harper's Ferry in Virginia was still fresh in the minds of slaveholders. Talk spread quickly throughout the South, that, if Abraham Lincoln was elected president, the southern states would leave the union. Southerners argued that if Lincoln was elected president, he would emancipate the slaves. Slaveholders wouldn't be compensated for their economic loss. This fear ran rapidly in the slave states. There was gossip on the plantation that blacks would be sent to South America, Central America, and to Liberia in Africa.

Massa Collins wanted to know if there was any agitation or unrest among his slaves. He had twenty-one slaves, twelve were males and nine were females. He felt his slaves were loyal to him. He commented to the slave holder Henry Miller at the slave auction in Savannah, that his slaves were happy. They laughed and joked but they are content Abraham remembered those words. Massa Collins should not fear any slave revolt from his twenty-one happy slaves. Massa Collins feared that if any of his slaves were to rebel against him it would be Abraham. He had been content for three years and he was married.

The older slaves on the plantation voiced their grievances against slavery. They had repeatedly said that slavery was morally wrong. Slavery was a sin and that sin would one day lead to the death of the institution. The Lord's hand was against slavery. He had delivered the Jews of old from bondage, and his fiery hand would deliver them from human bondage. Abraham proclaimed that slavery had divided the United States into Slave states and Free States. God would bring a plague upon the slave holders of the South just as he had upon the Egyptians. The slave holders would have to remove their chains and shackles and let them go. "Gawd's law is above all de laws. De good Lawd will 'sho dem jest like he did de 'gyptians of old" Abraham lamented.

"Ole Massa is 'fraid, dere is gwine to be a war. Abraham chuckled. "Dey knowed what happened in Virginny wid dat peacher' Nat Turner."

As the sun grew faint behind the tall pine trees, Abraham and Sunrise began to take their animals to the barn. It had been a cool day. A day that was full of surprises and weird behavior. Massa Collins had contradicted himself about the happy docile slave. At least in his mind, his idea began to challenge his thoughts.

Later that evening approaching dusk dark the African magic man showed up and knocked on Abraham's cabin door. As he reached his hand to open the door Abraham saw Isaac. "Come in

Isaac," Abraham said. "I ain't no African magic man,but what I do have will work." Abraham grinned.

"I don't know 'bout dat Abraham." I ain't no African magic man, but what I does will work magic." It saved my mammy and pappy from being sold into Bulloch County in 1843. Dey wuz from Marion County in Souse Caliny.

Isaac believed in magic and what they called herbs or roots. He gave Abraham a small brown bag full of crushed leaves. He instructed him to keep the little brown bag with him at all times. And when he returned to his cabin in the evening or at night let it rest on his chest. Abraham was instructed never to take the crushed leaves from the bag. "I'se passed by ole Massa and de overseer unnoticed earlier; dey never seed me" Isaac recalled. "It will ward off evil 'pirits too. Massa will never lay a whip on you again," Isaac said as he slowly walked out of the door.

The next day after Abraham and Sunrise returned from their day's task they sat down outside the cabin for a few minutes to rest. Seconds later they were joined by Henry, Isaac, and Charlie. Abraham cautioned the men not to let Massa Collins or his overseer see them. They were too suspicious of two of their fellow slaves. They were to be cautious at all times. Milly was now a cook at the big house but they were to have their first religious meeting. They would later call it their first solemn meeting on the plantation. They would work hard now to avoid Massa and his people from finding out where they worshipped. It was time they began their own divine service, the slaves murmured. "No moe dan fore of us can be seed in a group," Sunrise reminded everyone. "Hurry up we needs to git started soon."

Their first get together was brief, lasting for twelve minutes. The small group was careful not to be seen by the slave boss or the overseers. They quickly scattered and returned to their cabins after the signal to leave was clear. Soon the praises and prayers ended and the laughs and the somber occasion gave way to the stillness of night. Their first formal meeting was a success. Their major goal was to stay clear of Massa Collins and his overseers.

Three weeks later, thirty minutes after sunset a group of seven slaves met inside Sunrise's cabin. Abraham listened with awe and caution. Everyone listened as two men Sunrise and Charlie spoke for five minutes each. Then Henry and John spoke lastly, each for four minutes. They spoke of the New Jerusalem and crossing the Jordan River. They talked about the "Land of Milk and Honey. Everyone strongly felt that they'd soon be free to praise the Lord.

They knew the penalty if they were caught praying, reading, writing, or preaching about Jesus. The penalty was ten lashes for each slave and twenty lashes for the leader. They stationed a person to watch closely and give them the usual signal if anyone approached the area. The signal was a loud whistle one time then the sound of an owl.

The following morning a heavy rain fell and the field slaves were unable to work their assigned tasks. The rain fell in torrents for about an hour; then it rained intermittently for another hour. Abraham and Sunrise couldn't prepare the horses and mules for any kind of field work due to the boggy ground. "Massa Want us to clear some new ground. He tinking 'bout planting rice next year," Sunrise complained.

"Dis is de land for it. Massa says he needs land like dis. Where lots of water stands; rice grows. Last week, ole Massa talk 'bout getting more land for de cows to graze on." Henry said.

"Ole Massa crazy, dis land is for cotton and corn. 'Don't need more land for cows. Massa hab 'enuff' cows."

Two hours later Abraham, Sunrise and Henry were busy doing other tasks. The rain had completely stopped and they were busy cutting wood. Two trees had fallen down from the strong wind that accompanied the rain. Abraham was thinking about what he'd heard; the possibility of a slave uprising in the area. He knew Massa Collins had been talking with other slave owners in the region about the South going to war. This was sure to happen if Abraham Lincoln was elected president in November. He hadn't forgotten Sunrise's edict. Keep your ears open to what was being said by Massa Collins and the other white people.

Abraham thought about his two young children. Would slavery be abolished while his children were under the age of maturity? He knew there was a conflict between the slaveholding and non-slaveholding states. There was dissension over the issue of slavery in the United States Congress. There were growing debates and discord in the southern states as well.

An hour later the three men had finished cutting into pieces the two trees that had fallen down. They chopped the wood and stacked it in a place where the overseer had instructed them. The heavy rain prevented them from doing their regular assignment. And the three were happy for the distraction. The overseer stood closely by and watched every movement they made. Abraham began singing Charlie and Henry both were surprised, and shocked. They'd never heard him sing. His singing amused the rotund overseer who thought it was funny. Then Henry and Sunrise joined in the singing.

Later in the afternoon after their work had ended the three talked about what had transpired earlier that day. They were amused over each other's behavior in playing tricks on the startled overseer.

"I started singing 'cause de ole oberseer wuz being nosey. He messin' in what we is doin'." Abraham laughed.

"Us didn't know you could sing. Ain't heard you sing befo Abraham." Sunrise laughed standing to his feet. "Us fooled him, us is gwine to fool Massa too. Let em' tink we is crazy."

The next morning after Milly finished cooking breakfast at the big house. She had been the new cook for three months. She listened discreetly and undistracted to each word that was spoken coming from Massa and Missus and the other white folks that were in her presence. She heard most of the news that confronted the slave owners. She heard Massa Collins and Massa Tillman talk about a possible slave uprising in Liberty and McIntosh counties. It was being rumored daily that such a thing could happen. Milly kept her ears attuned as most of the slaves on the plantation did.

"Milly, I've got to go to the state capitol at Milledgeville. I want you to look after things while I'm away." Massa said.

"Yes suh, Massa I will. I'll take good care of tings." Milly said. I wonder what ole Massa is up to. Milly had heard him talk earlier about Milledgeville, Savannah, Macon, and other cities. But he'd been talking about Milledgeville lately. She wondered what Massa Collins was doing at that funny named place. She'd heard that's where they make laws for the state. They make laws there that affect all slaves in Georgia.

Later at midday when the bell rang for the slaves to come to dinner the sun shone hot. It was August and they were in the midst of harvesting their crops. The fields were soaked from a heavy rain that had fallen earlier. Abraham and Henry had just sat down and began to eat. Abraham mentioned to Henry about other work that Massa had planned ahead for them to do.

"Pretty soon Henry, we's got to clean up more land. I heard ole Massa tell Red jest de other day. Us's 'bout finished wid de crops," Abraham nodded to Henry

"Soon us will hab to cut moe wood for ole Massa. Dey will soon be finished wid dem two trees us cut," Henry said.

"'Yes, Henry, 'us will be finished befo' a heavy rain comes again. Massa is in no hurry. He tinks de Souse and de Nawth will soon be at war. Dey will be fighting ober us," Abraham laughed. I heard Massa talk wid Massa Eason de udder day. De slave states gwine to break apart from de Free states. "I heard de Souse is gwine to break away form de Union. Whatever dat means." Dey didn't 'spect I heard dem. And dey thought I didn't understand what dey was talkin' 'bout."

"And another ting Henry, if de wagons is torn up, and de mules and horses git sick we won't hab to work" Abraham laughed.

"Don't tink of it," Henry growled. You will git us all in trouble, Red will git de cowhide and whip de skin off our back."

A week later the mean rotund overseer was heard yelling at Abraham and the other slaves about clearing land for a road. The slaves had just eaten breakfast and were off to work a different task. They had axes, hoes, picks, shovels, and the tools necessary for clearing land for a road.

"Let's git to work and git this road built. Move on, you're moving too slow," Red shouted. He continued to yell and shout. The involuntary servants worked hard and unyielding. "This road has to be cleared by the end of the week." Without warning a tree limb split and hit Abraham on his left ankle. The impact knocked him to the ground. A huge limb split from the tree and fell on his ankle. The other slaves working with him quickly rushed in to remove the massive limb off Abraham's ankle. Henry, Charlie, John, and Isaac, were able to extricate him from the tree. Abraham's left leg and ankle quickly swelled up. A faint stream of blood slowly trickled down from his knee to his ankle.

Abraham hollered out in pain as he grabbed his left ankle. He grabbed a rag from his back pocket and pressed strongly against his ankle as Charlie and Henry stood over him as if sharing his pain. The ruthless overseer popped his whip and shouted "stay away from him, git back unless you want part of this cowhide." They jumped back as Abraham tried to stand but fell back. "He ain't hurt just lazy. This whip will cure any ailment." The crack of Red's whip could be heard throughout the slave quarters. The overseer's main concern was to clear the vegetation from the area for the building of the road.

Before the end of the work day Abraham was carried back to his cabin by Charlie and Henry. They were working about hundred yards from his cabin. Rilla was shocked when she saw what had happened to his leg. George was curious to know what happened to his father's leg and ankle. Rilla got a wooden bucket and poured it full of water. The bleeding had stopped, and the swelling from his leg had gone down. But his ankle was still swollen. He soaked his leg and ankle in warm water that was heated by Rilla. Before he went to bed she rubbed cold grease on the sore part.

Later that night Abraham had trouble falling asleep. He got out of bed and staggered on his right foot toward the door. Then he returned to bed. He was quiet and didn't mumble a word to anyone. Rilla just stirred at the small dim lamp light that burned slowly on the table. "Rilla, give me dat bag of leaves the African magic man gave me; I'll put the bag on my chest. Abraham slept with the bag on his chest and Rilla attended to his ankle during the night. She applied the horse salve to his ankle.

The next morning the bell rang for the slaves to begin work. "We are going to finish this road or we'll work Saturday and Sunday. I told you earlier, so stop dragging around. Y'all do understand what I am saying, don't you?"

"Yes suh boss, us does under'tand." Henry and Sunrise worked hurriedly to cut down the vegetation. The men struggled to remove the small trees and branches that hindered their progress. Roots had to be dug up, cut, and placed in a pile on the far side of the cleared land.

Abraham's leg and ankle were still sore the swelling had gone down. Much of the pain had eased during the night. He was given a new task of shelling corn. He didn't have to stand and this relieved the strain from his foot and ankle. Rilla placed cold grease and found a spider's web to place on the wound. Abraham worked tireless at his new assignment. Shelling corn was less painful than using an axe or hoe on an infirm leg and ankle.

After lunch the slaves returned to work clearing the land for the completion of the road. Abraham limped back to the barn to continue his new job of shelling corn. He was beginning to enjoy his new task. His leg and ankle was feeling better. He began thinking to himself whether the overseer and Massa Collins would return him to clearing land for the new road. Outside the other slaves continued their forced labor, clearing the land for the road.

They worked Saturday to finish building the road. Rilla reminded Abraham that the new road was a blessing for them. Now they would be able to track the movements of Massa Collins and his visiting white friends more clearly. "De Lawd 'sho is good Abraham. You can see ole Massa when he comes and goes" Rilla smiled. 'Special on Saddy and Sunday; dey come and goes. Dey is 'fraid dat sometin' is gwine to happen.

"De old sheriff was dere yesditty; I seed 'em hand ole Massa a piece of paper. Massa looked at it den give it back to 'em. Massa didn't know I seed 'em, he looked as if one of his hosses' had died."

Abraham and Rilla observed that Massa Collins spent the next two weeks within the county. He stayed within the boundaries of his plantation. He waited anxiously to see whether Georgia would secede from the union. Talk had strengthened about a secession convention to be held in Milledgeville. Georgia would soon determine whether to leave the union or remain loyal to the republic. Massa Collins was unaware that Abraham and the others could see more clearly his movements and activities that transpired daily on the plantation. The completion of the new road provided a better view for Abraham and the other slaves from their cabins.

Three months later in November 1860 Abraham Lincoln was elected president of the United States. With the election of Abraham Lincoln South Carolina was the first Southern state to secede from the Union. Massa Collins and the slaveholders across the state became uneasy as they struggled with the reality of the emancipation freeing of their slaves. The slaveholders across the south feared the loss of their human chattel would bring them economic ruin. The slaves understood the gravity of the secession crisis and their owners realized that slavery's demise was inevitable. Abraham, Rilla, and Milly perceived that the winds of rebellion had begun to blow strongly across Georgia. The foundation upon which the South's economic structure rested was threatened and had begun to wither.

Abraham and the other slaves were thrilled to learn of the election of Abraham Lincoln as president of the United States. They sensed that a change was going to take place on the southern plantations in Georgia and the rest of the South.

Chapter Eight

On a cold December day in 1860 Abraham, Sunrise, and Charlie had just returned from digging up stumps. They sat down outside of Abraham's cabin. A paper fell from Abraham's shirt. "Where did you git dat paper from?" Sunrise snapped.

"I took it from Massa Collins buggy. I saw ole Massa get out of the buggy; den I seed dis paper and ole Massa jest left it dere I sneaked over dere and got it."

"Don talk like dat Abraham. Massa Collins catch you wid dat paper he'll sell all of us." Sunrise warned Abraham.

"I knows, us ain't 'spose to hab any books, paper, or nuttin' like dat. Massa see us wid any ting like dat he will give us fifteen lashes or sell us poor slaves to 'nother Massa" Abraham laughed.

The next day after the bell sounded for the slaves to come to dinner Massa Collins was waiting to talk to them. He knew that secession from the union was inevitable. South Carolina was within days of leaving the union; and the other slaveholding states would soon follow. Massa Collins knew that he had to do something before Georgia left the union.

"I want all of you to listen to me. We may soon be in a war with the North" he told them. You do know what a war is. The slaves looked submissive as they stared at Massa Collins and nodded their head in agreement. If we lose the war, you will be sold to President

Abraham Lincoln in the North. He will take all of you away from each other and you won't see one another again. There won't be anything I can do. The one hour break for dinner came to a close and the bell rang for them to return to work. Abraham, Sunrise, and Charlie returned to digging up stumps for the clearing and preparation of new ground.

Abraham began to think of all the things that related to his survival as an involuntary servant. He thought of the conversation he had with Sunrise about the piece of paper he took from Massa Collins buggy. He heard the echo of Sunrise's voice in his ear. Don't let Massa Collins see you with that paper. Get rid of that paper or he will give you fifteen lashes. Abraham reflected on the cruelties and barbarity associated with slavery.

Later that afternoon he thought of what Sunrise had told him. But he had something to say to him. "When I first arrived at Massa Collins place, you talked 'bout niggers in dis state run away to Florida. Dem niggers left Georgia and joined dem Injuns. Some of 'em even married dem Injun women."

"Jest 'spose Massa heard you talk 'bout dese tings. And he wanted to know who told you dese tings. And Massa gits mighty mad wid you. Massa gits so mad wid you and wants to know who learnt you all dem tings. 'Spose he asks, how could a nigger know all dese tings that can't read or write."

"What do you tell ole Massa, Sunrise?"

"I'se won't tell 'em a ting. I won't let ole Massa hear me say nuttin'," Sunrise laughed.

Abraham thought of Massa Collins seeking revenge and retaliation against his slaves. He knew of the false tensions and rumors that circulated on the plantation about a slave uprising. The slaveholders had the law on their side. Slave codes harshly punished blacks that threaten to violate any of these laws. The slaveholders had the backing of the United States to enforce the Fugitive slave Act. Abraham squirmed at the thought of being sold away from Massa Collins plantation. The slave owner had the bloodhounds and the whip to punish unruly slaves. Abraham knew that his greatest challenge lay ahead. He thought of the newly elected president, Abraham Lincoln. What would President Lincoln do to free him and his people from bondage?

Abraham listened to the problems that surrounded the slavery issue. He kept his ears open. But did he really understand the words spoken by the whites on the plantation. He thought to himself, secession, secede, and John Brown's attack on Harper's ferry. What did those things mean to him?

Later that night Abraham was thinking as he talked to Rilla. Little George and Harriet were fast asleep. "Sunrise asks me today 'bout de paper I gots dat 'blongs to ole Massa." Abraham said reaching for the dipper to get a drink of water.

"What paper?" Rilla asked.

Dat paper I'se got out of Massa Collins' buggy. I seed 'em when he left de buggy and went in de big house."

"Dat's de paper he gives to de sherif'. But de sherif' give it back to 'em," Rilla explained.

"Sunrise was 'fraid ole Massa or Red wid give me fifteen lashes. Abraham quipped.

"I tink it's an 'portant paper. Massa been talkin' 'bout it since de udder day. Dat paper hab sometin' to do wid land Massa been talkin' 'bout. Massa and ole Massa Eason been talking 'bout buyin' and sellin' niggers. I'se heard dem Abraham."

Rilla and Abraham continued to talk about Massa Collins and the things they'd heard him and the other slave owners talk and discuss. "If de Souse leaves de union and wins de war, us will still be Massa Collins slaves."

"No Rilla, President Lincoln is gwine to set us free." Ole Massa n' nem' is 'fraid. Massa walks 'round like he's been kicked by ole Bob. Dat ole mule 'sho is crazy;" Abraham laughed.

"No, Abraham, Massa act's like he hit his head on a 'rock. I seed 'em jest yedditty, walking 'round struttin' like a Wooster wid his hed cut off."

"All dis talk' 'bout us slaves turnin' 'gainst dey massas'. Dat kind of talk hab ole Massa 'fraid of his shadow," Abraham guffawed.

The next morning the bell rang for the slaves to get ready for work. The male slaves had been chopping wood and digging up stumps. The female slaves were busy washing and scrubbing dirty clothes and cleaning the Massa's house. Milly and Rilla were the cooks and harvested the vegetables from the winter garden. The slaves worked their assigned tasks until the bell rang for them to come to dinner. After dinner they continued their designated work. The overseers Red and Smith watched Abraham and the rest of the slaves as they performed the work assigned them.

The election of Abraham Lincoln served as a catalyst for heightened tensions between the North and the South. South Carolina had seceded from the Union and other Southern states had planned to follow her lead. Whatever the outcome between the North and the South over the secession crisis, Abraham and the other slaves were prepared to see what action president Lincoln and the North would take.

Among the slaves on the Collins plantation Abraham exhibited the most courage. He knew that in his attempt to escape to freedom, if he was unsuccessful he would face the whip and be castigated as an unmanageable slave. He knew that he could be hunted down by paddy rollers or slave catchers. His punishment could be harsh and extreme. And the anguish of being sold away from his family hammered his mind daily.

Abraham thought about what he'd do if there was a slave uprising in his county. Was his county too small to entertain the thought of a slave rebellion? The small slave population in Tattnall County and surrounding counties would be too weak and defenseless against the slaveholders and the provincial government that sanctioned slavery. He thought that all the laws and slave codes were against an illiterate army of slaves.

The secession crisis was a major issue and topic on farms and plantations in Georgia. Georgia and Southern Democrats were divided with Northern Democrats over the issue of secession. Slavery would become the leading issue that was a part of every slaveholder's conversation in the South and the state of Georgia for the next four years.

Georgia's delegates met at the secession Convention in Milledgeville on January 19, 1861, and voted to make Georgia an independent state. South Carolina became the first state to secede from the Union. Later, Mississippi, Florida, and Alabama seceded from the Union on January 26, 1861. And on February 2, 1861 Texas left the Union.

On February 4, 1861 Abraham and Rilla's third child was born. It was a cold hazy morning when the midwife, Alice delivered the tiny baby girl. The baby was delivered three hours before the bell sounded for the slaves to begin work. It was a joyous occasion for Abraham and Rillia. They named the newborn Macy Ann instead of Amanda, Milly's sister.

It was already five months into the New Year. Abraham Lincoln had already been inaugurated president of the United States. Confederate forces fired upon Fort Sumter in Charleston harbor taking over the federal fort. Massa Collins and the slaveholders in the area had felt for a long time that war was inevitable. Abraham and Sunrise heard Massa Collins and Massa Eason say they knew that South Carolina would be the first Southern state to secede.

Abraham had been married now for three years. He and Rilla with the birth of their new baby had three small children. Abraham thought of their safety day and night. He faced a dilemma. If he tried to escape and was captured or killed; what would happen to his wife and children? They would be without a husband and father. His last attempt to run away was before his marriage to Rilla in 1857. How much longer could he endure being the property of another? Being a slave he had no rights which white people respected. The great documents of freedom he thought did not apply to him and the other slaves. The Dred Scott decision had declared that black people were property and had no rights which were to be respected by white people.

He spoke to his three children. "You ain't gwine to be no slave." He picked up George and held him in his arms. "By the time you gits to be five, de good Lawd is gwine to set us free." Abraham spoke as little George remained silent staring in his eyes. "And you, little Harriet, you is gwine to be great! You won't be no slave fer Massa Collins. I prays to de Lawd ebery day and night dat you chilun' be free." He put George down slowly and rubbed his head.

Abraham looked at Rilla and then looked at little Macy Ann. He thought to himself; he wished his mother could see his three children. He didn't know if she was dead or alive. He'd had these thoughts before. He didn't know if she was a slave on a plantation or farm in Georgia or South Carolina. His thoughts were vexing to him. He was thinking that President Lincoln would do something to bring an end to slavery. He'd heard Massa Collins talking to other people about President Lincoln and the abolitionist from the North. He didn't understand everything they said, but he knew that something was going to happen soon.

Later that night Milly came to their cabin to bring Rilla a head cloth. "I heard the people in the North and the South is tryin' to kill each other. Old Massa is 'scarid. Thanks de Lawd us won't be slaves much longer."

"De good Lawd is on our side. President Lincoln took all de chains and shackles of de slaves. And we was free."

"Spose de Souse wins dis war. Den us will be slaves of Massa Collins forever. Our chilun'will be old Massa's slaves." Rilla mumbled.

"No Rilla, don' talk dat way. We'll soon be livin' in de land of milk and honey."

The next day it rained all morning. Heavy intermittent rain showers fell until early afternoon. The plants in the field were drenched and cracks were cut across rows uprooting some of the plants. Both cotton and corn plants were damaged by the abundant rainfall. Abraham, Sunrise, and Charlie retired to work in the barn after it was too wet to work in the field. The excessive water left the area boggy and slippery; it was too wet for the animal to walk in or the wagons to move forward.

The slaves went to work in the barn shoveling animal manure. Abraham and Sunrise were given the task of shelling corn. And Charlie was joined by Henry and Joseph in loading compost on the wagons. The overseer strolled closer to the barn, as the slaves worked to complete their tasks. A light rain continued to fall and the day passed slowly as the involuntary servants steadily worked.

"Y'all ain't moving fast enough," howled the vile overseer. He limped around his left foot. "Massa Collins said you must finish this work. Tomorrow, we have something else for you to do. Do you understand what I'm saying?" Abraham and Charlie looked at each then at Henry and Joseph. The scent from the compost was as potent as the outhouses on the plantation. As they moved closer, the overseer grabbed his shotgun with his right hand and his whip with his left. "Stop!" he yelled. "Don't come any closer." "He was shaking as he spoke and his voice quivered." The rumor of a possible slave uprising was still fresh in the slaveholders' mind. The work day soon came to an end as they finished their task for the day.

Three days later the ground was dry enough for the wagons to move over the land without bogging down. Abraham worked with the cooper Sampson. Joseph and Charlie helped them haul casks from the blacksmith shop to a specified location. The new overseer felt that the slaves were working too slowly. His voice cracked as he spoke. Fear and anticipation of the unknown clouded his thoughts. He was told the slaves on the Collins plantation were submissive and docile. No problems had recurred since Abraham's last attempt to escape three years earlier in 1858. All was quiet except for rumors that were circulating about a possible slave rebellion. A slave uprising had occurred in Laurens County a few years back. The slaveholders were placed on alert in Liberty, McIntosh, Burke, and in Jefferson Counties because of their large concentration of slaves in the areas.

"The boss, Mr. Collins is going to sell all of you. Those of you who ain't working hard, Mr. Collins is going to get shed of you. He is going to take you to that market in Savannah." The tall thin overseer spoke in a harsh tone. He had been working a little less than three weeks. Red had been working for two years on the Tippins plantation. He became sick and moved to Bulloch County just before the new overseer came.

"Do you know what happened to them old mules where I cam from?" My boss had me to burn them up. Why? Because they'd become too lazy and wouldn't work. We didn't sell them. No! We put the fire to them." Abraham and Charlie wondered if he was telling the truth, or was scared out of his wits. The tall lean man continued to yell and holler, popping his brown cowhide. The slaves continued working until the end of the day. The bell sounded for them to return to the slave quarters. Another forced work day had come to an end.

An hour later Abraham, Charlie, Joseph, Milliy, and Alice, the midwife chose to have a few minutes of praise service to give thanks to God. They as always had to carefully select their time and place to give thanks. Sunrise and Henry watched for the overseer and any paddy rollers that might be in the area.

"Where is Sampson?" Abraham asked, grasping his hands together. "He sho' ought'a be here. That man is always late." Abraham thought.

"If us don' smell anything, Sampson ain't 'round." Joseph snickered.

"He's de tanner, you talkin' 'bout. Dat's John; he can't be trusted. He's one of old Massa Collins niggers." Milly exclaimed.

They were to have a short worship service and rush back to the slave quarters before they were missed. They didn't want to raise any suspicion or warn anyone as to what they were doing. Sunrise and Henry surveyed the area carefully and alertly in every direction. Abraham and Charlie knew what happened to the slave preacher on Massa Smith's plantation. He was given twenty lashes for having a worship service without Massa Smith's permission.

The slave worship service came to an end twenty minutes after they started. Sunrise gave the all clear signal for everyone to return to their slave cabins. For the third straight time they worshipped God without any interruption from the overseer, paddy rollers, or Massa Collins. Everyone felt good about what had happened.

The time had come for the slaves to have another frolic on the plantation. Because of past problems of slave rebellions on plantations in Virginia and South Carolina, slaveholders were fearful of slave uprisings. The slaves knew of the tension that existed in the county and in surrounding areas.

Early the next morning the bell rang for the slaves to return to work. It was the second to the last work day of the week for them. The overseer had a special task for them to carry out. Shortly after breakfast, Abraham, Henry, and Charlie were instructed to help Sampson. Their job was to load barrels of corn on the large wagon to be hauled to Massa Tillman's farm three miles away. This was an important task that needed to be done. Abraham wondered why the three of them were chosen to help Sampson. Later that morning they completed hauling two wagon loads of casks full of corn in each barrel. The trip to and from the Tillman plantation was an all day journey. The cold November wind-chilled day had zapped the energy from Henry, Charlie, Abraham, and Sampson. The titan cooper, Sampson showed discomfort from working in the frigid temperature.

Chapter Nine

One week after the issuance of the Emancipation Proclamation the news reached the Collins plantation. It was a jubilant day for all the slaves on the plantation. The news of their freedom was the happiest day of their lives.

"Hallelujah! Hallelujah! Abraham us is free," shouted Sunrise. President Lincoln hab issued dat law." Sunrise continued to sing and dance. All of the slaves on the Collins plantation were animate and jubilant. They knew something had happened. They saw the reaction of the slave owners to the news of the Emancipation Proclamation. The former slaves sang and danced all morning after the news of their freedom from bondage arrived on the Collins plantation.

This day was one of the coldest days in the month of January. But the slaves had a warm feeling in their hearts all morning after receiving the joyous news. Abraham prayed and thanked the Lord for this day. "Gawd, you heard our prayers; we thanks you fer dis day. I thanks de Lawd, dat my little chilun won't grow up in bondage. Dey won't be sold away from us, we thanks you Lawd. No moe lashes on my back. Bressed be thou name Lawd." Everyone stood around and listened as Abraham prayed. The former slaves continued to sing and dance.

"Us is free, but what does us do. Where does us go?" Charlie cried out looking at Abraham. Us doesn't hab any land, hosses, mules, and no plows. Charlie said.

"De good Lawd will make a way. He will lead us to de new Jerusalem. He will bring de North Star right here on Massa Collins place to guide us." Abraham said looking up in the sky toward heaven.

"I'se knows dat's de truth Abraham. Us ain't no animals or no property, us is all made in de image of de good Lawd." He will one day bring a plague 'gainst dese evil people. He don' put de pen in President Lincoln's hand to set us free."

"We need to thank de Lawd for what he hab done." Abraham said. His head stretched upward toward the sky. The former slaves wasted no time in giving thanks to the Lord and to praise him in what they called "de triumph of good over evil." The God of Abraham, Isaac, and Jacob had answered their prayers.

Later that afternoon the celebration continued. The former slaves met outside the cabin of Abraham and Rilla to continue their celebration. Some of them were superstitious and believed the Emancipation Proclamation was a trick to further enslave them. Others clung to their rabbit foot and turkey feathers as the celebration continued. Abraham and Charlie dismissed such behavior as the work of the devil. Even Henry was cautious about the former slaves celebrating their freedom.

An hour later, just before dusk dark they had another prayer to thank God for liberating them from bondage. Adam, the oldest of the former slaves prayed and gave thanks to the Lord. At sixty-five and stoop-shouldered he could hardly see. "Lawd, we's been here in de land of bondage fer a long time. We tanks you fer takin' de shackles from our feets and legs. Lawd, bress us yo' chilun', dis day. Bress each and ebery one of us. Bress us from de rain, from de cold weather, and de heat. Lawd, may we see our bressed luv ones who was sold away. Lawd, may us soon find dem. Bress us dis day and night oh Gawd our Lawd who hab saved us and our chilun' Amen"

The next morning Master Collins met with his former slaves in front of his house to talk to them. "I want you all to know that what I was doing was for your own good. I was just trying to show you how to work and have something." He was nervous as his voice cracked trying to explain to them the good deeds of slavery. He reiterated what he said before. "I know that you worked hard, but I wanted you to have something. And learn the importance of hard work."

"All of you had plenty to eat and you were never hungry. You had clothes on your back and shoes on your feet. When you didn't obey my orders some of you were beaten with the whip of correction. One or two of you tried to run away, to escape from the good things you had here. Those old Northern Yankees intruded on us, and they meddled in our way of life. They will pay for it."

"I know you don't have any place to go; you can stay on here with me. It will be planting time soon and you can just go on doing to the same as you were before." His voice had dwindled to almost a whisper.

"We knows dat Massa Collins, but all we wants is our freedom. And what we wants is to be free from de whip. We will stay on if we is given a piece of de land to work." Abraham looked up at his former slave owner who appeared uneasy and cautious. "Another ting Massa, I wants my name to be Abraham Jackson. I wants to be called by dat name and I wants my wife and chillum to be called Jackson."

This statement brought disapproval form some of the former slaves as they looked away as to disassociate themselves from what Abraham had just said. Massa Collins looked stunned and there was silence for about two minutes. Both Massa Collins and the others were stunned by that statement. Abraham had been severely beaten during slavery for refusing to acknowledge Collins as his last name.

Later that night, Abraham thought of all the things his former slave boss had said to them and wanted to consider the options. He faced a dilemma. The choice he made would have a profound effect upon his life for years to come. He thought of his present circumstances and what lay ahead for his future. He asked Rilla: "Does we stay on wid Massa Collins, or do we move on and look fer another place. What does you tink Rilla?" Abraham asked placing his hand on the back of his head.

The next morning shortly before breakfast Abraham motioned for the children and Rilla to form a circle around him as he prayed. The old slave bell didn't ring for the first time in decades. Abraham hesitated, waiting for the sound of the bell before he gave thanks to God. "We thank de O God fer yo' mercy. Dis is a great day O Lawd, no mo' will us be bought and sold like hosses and cows. Our little one's will hab no Massas' Lawd. You is our only Massa Lawd. We tank de bressed Jesus. Amen."

Minutes later Abraham, Sunrise, Charlie and Henry went to talk to Massa Collins about the land he had promised to give them. They saw Massa talking with Sampson and two other former slaves. "Old Massa promised to gibe us five acres of land. Dat is if us stay's on wid 'em. Dat is if we stay on fer two years and clear dat land down by de creek." Charlie said pointing to the right of them."

"We is free now, we don' hab to do nuttin' fer old Massa. It'll take us a long time to clear dat land. We is got to cut all of dem trees down and drag de big ones out."

"Dat's right Henry. We cut de trees down and old Massa may give dem to us. Dat is if we stay's on wid him," Abraham declared.

The sun had fully risen as they approached the Collins house. They appeared happy and full of energy. "Massa Collins, Abraham spoke saying "I'se will stay on if us gets de five acres."

"I told you people the other day, that I'd give five acres to anyone who stayed on with me. Do you understand? Five free acres of land and tools to work the land." The former slave owner was growing impatient with his former slaves. He'd heard earlier that morning that a few of them were talking about going to Savannah. He heard that Sunrise and Charlie were going to Virginia in search of their parents and siblings who were sold away from them in 1845. They wanted to make a new start as well.

The next morning Abraham met with his former slave owner to receive the farm tools he was promised. He waited for Sunrise and Charlie to meet with him but they didn't show up. Henry showed up just after Abraham received his designated five acres of land and his farm tools. After Abraham was shown the land he was going to farm, he returned to gather all of his tools. He was given one of the farm mules by the new overseer.

Later that evening Abraham spoke to Sunrise and Charlie; neither of whom was married. Sunrise talked to Abraham about what he was going to do. Abraham tried to anticipate what Sunrise and Charlie were going to talk about. He knew their situation was similar to his.

"I knows Abraham where I'se gwine and what I'se got to do. I hears you and 'nem others don' know what you is gwine to do. I goin' back to old Viginny. Dat's where my old grand pappy comes from. And his grand pappy was from Africa, a place dey calls de Gold Coast." I'se going to git me a new name and make a new start for myself."

"What will your new name be? What will you call yoself Sunrise? Abraham asked. I could go to another place too Sunrise. But I is gwine to work dis five acre piece of land Massa gives me. I is gwine to save a dollar or two, then I'se gwine to buy me five mo' acres of land. The Yankee soldiers will be here soon. What was yo' name befo' Massa gives you his name," Abraham asked.

"I doesn't know, I was sold from old Viginny along wid some othe yung' chillum. Dat was back in 1845. I listened to what my grand pappy said to me." Sunrise said.

"Well Charlie, what is you gwine to do?" Abraham asked.

"Us ain't neber seed Massa Lincoln. But sometin' is happin'. Massa Lincoln is a buckra jest like Massa Collins. Ain't he like dem white folk dat made us slaves Abraham?" Dey say us is like de hosses, cows,and mules." I is gwine to Florida; Dat's to de south of us. I is gwine to live wid the Seminole Injuns." Dem Injuns don' hab slaves Abraham."

"Dat was a long time ago when de Indians were free of de buckra. Tings is different now. De Seminoles is no longer de rulers. I thought 'bout running away down dere. Ain't no niggers chief of dem Seminoles anymore. Dem buckra is in charge now." Abraham lectured Charlie.

"Do you tink you can git by dem paddy rollers, Charlie? Massa Lincoln hab told all de slave owners in dis state and de other states dat hab slaves us is free. But dem old paddy rollers is still hunting us."

"I'se knows dat Massa Lincoln ain't no Nat Turner or Dat Vessey man. Dey tried to set de slaves free. I heard dem niggers in dat Liberty County and in dat Burke and McIn . . . tosh counties was gwine to fight dere slave Massas'. I heard dat befo' Massa Lincoln set us free."

Three months later in June, Abraham had finished the crops he'd planted. He had planted corn and vegetables on the land he'd received. He was given a mule and two plows to use to break up and cultivate the ground. He received everything he needed to attend the land and get off to a good start. Rilla's brother's were old enough to help Abraham work his land. Frank had just turned fourteen and Henry was eleven.

A month later in the latter part of June Abraham heard two men engaged in a conversation in the barn. He listened carefully to their conversation. James told Massa Collins that nigger soldiers had attacked the white citizens and burned the town of Darien. This carnage had taken place two weeks earlier. The white citizens of the community were devastated by the destruction of property in their town. This was the first time Abraham had heard of black troops engaged in fighting in Georgia. He was so amazed to hear this news that he was unable to work the rest of the day.

Later that evening Abraham talked to Sampson and Noah what he heard Massa Collins and Massa Tillman talking about. The slaves knew about the war that was taking place between the North and the South. They'd heard about the major battles that were fought. They knew about the Altamaha River and the coastal town of Darien.

"You boys won't believe what I'se heard old Massa talk 'bout dis day. He told Massa Tillman dat nigger sojers burnt de town of Darien two weeks ago." Abraham said with a grin on his face.

"Abram, I ain't knowed dat dey were colored sojers fightin' de rebs in dis state. I'se jes' as shocked as de buckra. I'se heard President Lincoln was gwine to hab colored sojers back in April."

"De good Lawd don' heard our prayers. I had hope de Lawd would soon deliver us from bondage. Old Massa 'nem tinks dat de Yankee sojers will soon be here."

Chapter Ten

Seven months later in January 1864 Abraham and Rilla had just celebrated the birth of their fourth child, Lewis born on December 7, 1863. The New Year was ushered in by the celebration of Emancipation Day. It had been a year and five days since President Lincoln issued the Emancipation Proclamation. The problem of slavery still plagued President Abraham Lincoln and the Border States. His presidential decree did not affect a single slave in the loyal Border States.

George, Abraham and Rilla's oldest child celebrated his fifth birthday on January 5th. The day was celebrated by merrymaking and much prayer. This continued for most of the day as the former slaves exchanged stories and tales about the hard times in shackles and chains. Abraham's festive spirit soon turned to gloom as he reflected on what had happened to his mother and two brothers in South Carolina. He didn't know what had happened to them. He wondered if they were still alive or had been sold within the state of South Carolina or to another slave state.

Three months later in April Abraham continued to work the land that was given to him by his former slave owner. He and the other former slaves that stayed on were learning about the status of the military and the war effort from the talk of their former slave owners. Abraham kept his eyes open and his ears attuned to what was being said. Sunrise was no longer among the former slaves that stayed on with Massa Collins. It was rumored that he went back to Virginia. That was the talk among the slaves. It was a dangerous time for a black man to travel in the South. Things were changing for the Confederacy as they began to retreat. Union soldiers were marching from Tennessee into Georgia. The South was in dire need of men and supplies. Abraham and Charlie were talking about what they heard when they were unloading compost two days earlier.

"Massa Jeff Davis talkin' 'bout using colored soldiers to fight 'gainst de North." Henry grinned.

"They were talking 'bout using colored men befo' President Lincoln set us free. Dey was talking 'bout using colored men to build roads, dig ditches, and as cooks for de rebel sojers. I heard old Massa say dat de other day Henry. Those rebels is confused. When you bump yo' big toe it hurts. De toe aches and yo' whole body aches. Slavery is de big toe. It causes de Souse to ache. De Souse, cause de Nawth and de whole nation to ache." Abraham rambled.

"De South is trying to make wrong right and right wrong. Dat kind of tinking is jest like grass blowin' in de wind."

Later in the year, in September, General William T. Sherman and his armies burned Atlanta and began their notorious march toward Savannah. General Joe Johnston and his confederate army was no match for Sherman's armies as the general employed his "scorched earth policy." Sherman's armies burned the city of Atlanta and began destroying plantation and farms throughout the state.

Abraham and the other slaves had heard about Sherman's oncoming march and the carnage and destruction his armies caused. They captured horses, mules, hogs, and everything that southern plantation owners and farmers had. The slaves on these farms and plantations were thrilled at seeing the oncoming Yankee soldiers.

Two months later, in November plantation owners became more fearful as General Sherman's armies moved closer to their objective of capturing Savannah. Massa Collins knew of the destructive path Sherman's armies were taking en route to the sea. The closer General Sherman marched toward Washington, Jefferson, Burke, and Jenkins Counties the more frightened the slave owners became. Massa Collins instructed Abraham, Henry, and the other former slaves to hide his valuables and burn the cotton and other goods he had stored. His three smokehouses were stuffed with hams, cured meats, and other goods.

"Massa Collins," Abraham spoke, a candid look on his face. "President Lincoln's sojers knows us ain't got no slaves and us doesn't own any land. I don't want his sojers to bother us. Befo' dey gets here" Us will hide all of yo valuables."

"Those soldiers won't attack any of you. They are going to punish me and the other plantation owners. They are going to destroy my animals and burn my smokehouse and take our china and silverware. I heard what they did to those poor people in Atlanta and Milledgeville."

Abraham and the other former slaves were elated that Sherman's armies were liberating Georgia and the African American people who'd been enslaved for well over a century. He knew that the angel of the Lord had marched with Sherman's armies freeing his people. Many of the former slaves that had worked for years on southern farms and plantations followed General Sherman on his march through Georgia. The soldiers in blue were a welcome sight for many African American men and women.

In June of 1863 Union soldiers of the Fifty-Fourth Massachusetts and the Second South Carolina Volunteers burned the town of Darien in Georgia. The First South Carolina Volunteers led an expedition up the Altamaha River before Union forces attacked Atlanta. Many slaves left the area with the First South Carolina Volunteers and joined their ranks as soldiers.

In December 1864 General Sherman completed his march to the sea arriving in Savannah and presenting the city of Savannah to President Abraham Lincoln as a Christmas present. General Sherman also included thousands of bales of cotton and a hundred plus guns.

Chapter Eleven

With the issuance of President Lincoln's Emancipation Proclamation Northern abolitionists called for the enlistment of African American soldiers into the union army. Abraham and the slaves on the Collins plantation had waited for General Sherman's armies to arrive in the Southeastern part of the state. Two years had passed since the issuance of the Emancipation Proclamation and it was time for Abraham to make a decision.

Two months later Abraham was told that the Union army needed former slaves to fight against the rebel forces. That night after the children were asleep he told her his intentions. "Rilla I'se got something to tell you. I been thinking 'bout it all day. I'll soon be going to Savannah to join Abe Lincoln's army. I doesn't know when de war will be over. George is now six; and yo' brother Frank is fifteen and Henry is thirteen. Your momma and Henry and his wife will help out. Dere ain't no need to worry none. Abe Lincoln's sojers is everywhere all over de land."

At first Rilla was afraid for Abraham to leave her and the small children. Abraham assured her that she and the children would be taken care of while he was away. Abraham bade good-bye to Rilla and the Children on a cold February day in 1865. His shoes were raggedy and full of holes. His coat and shirt were worn and had holes in both the shirt and coat. He had an old worn brown hat. He found Savannah to be a large city swarming with black soldiers and new recruits eager to enlist in the Union army.

The Thirty-Third Regiment of United States Colored Troops had been in Charleston, South Carolina since February. They arrived in Savannah the second week in March. Abraham and the other former slaves were to enlist for a period of three years. A month later in April 1865 Abraham was a new recruit with Company C of the Thirty-Third Regiment formerly the First South Carolina Volunteers. He had mixed feeling about his enlistment as he spoke to Jeremiah.

"Don't know 'bout leaving de wife and chilun'. I'se been thinking 'bout how Massa gwine to treat them." Abraham said.

"Abraham, yo' old boss is somewhere hiding." New soldier: jest think about the bonus you is gwine to get. The thirteen dollars per month you is gwine to get will make you happy." Jeremiah grinned.

"What is you gwine to do when de war is over Jeremiah?" You gwine back to yo' old boss, when de war is over?" I ain't ever gwine to be a slave again for no white man. We gwine to beat all dem rebels," Abraham laughed.

"Guess what de first thing I'se gwine to learn to do Jeremiah. I'se going to learn to write and spell my name. I ain't no Abraham Collins no more, I'se Abraham Jackson. Yes, Jeremiah, I'se is gwine to learn to read and write."

Later that day, Abraham and Jeremiah heard the words from the lieutenant they'd been waiting to hear.

"Sergeant: Yes sir, lieutenant. Make sure these new recruits get uniforms and boots. Sergeant, these new recruits deserve the best. They are no longer the property of other men. They are soldiers with the Thirty-Third."

"Can you read or write your name," the sergeant asked Abraham.
"No sir."

"Make your mark here for your name." The sergeant exclaimed pointing to the bottom of the paper. "After you finish the company surgeon will examine you."

The lieutenant, Nelson S. White called for the men to move to the back to be examined by the surgeon. The company surgeon looked carefully across the backs of the men for scars as all of the men had scars from previous whippings from their former masters or overseers.

The new recruits were men of diverse physical descriptions. Abraham was short and muscular built. He was strong and powerful with brown eyes and black wooly hair. Jeremiah was a tall wiry man, close to six feet tall He'd been beaten by his Massa in November 1862 for stealing sweet potatoes; six weeks before Abraham Lincoln issued the Emancipation Proclamation. These recruits had grown tough and thick-skinned under the brutality of bondage.

Abraham was twenty-eight years of age. Most of the recruits were in their late twenties; many followed Sherman's armies into Savannah. They were courageous African American men with a common goal to free themselves and their families from a life of bondage.

Abraham's first week as a soldier he thought of his wife and four small children he'd left back on the Collins plantation. The first few nights seemed to grow longer as he thought of their safety and well-being. His oldest son was now six years of age and he knew that his father had left to join the army to fight against those who'd enslaved them. After his first week in uniform Abraham began to feel better. He was now a man and not the property of his former slaveholder.

Lieutenant White spoke to the new recruits about learning to read and write. "You men will be given the opportunity to learn to read and write your name. You will be taught by the company chaplain. You will be given instruction when you're not on guard or provost duty. The chaplain has all the information for you. You will also learn how to spell and do simple arithmetic. Before you return to civilian life you'll have a full knowledge of what's needed to become literate."

The news of the surrender of General Robert E. Lee to General Ulysses S. Grant at Appomattox Courthouse in Virginia was met with elation and a feeling of gloom. Abraham had joined up to fight against the rebels and now how could he since the South had surrendered. The bitter struggle and sectional conflict which divided the country into North and South and slave states and Free states had come to an end. Surrender at Appomattox meant triumph and victory for the former slaves and defeat and dishonor for the Confederacy.

Five days after the war ended tragic news of the assassination of President Lincoln brought painful and disturbing news to the Thirty-Third Regiment. The men were saddened by the heartbreaking news of the assassination of President Lincoln by John Wilkes Booth, a Confederate sympathizer. It was President Lincoln who had issued the Emancipation Proclamation in January of 1863 upon military necessity. His actions paved the way for the voluntary enlistment of African American recruits.

"Dey don' kilt de President of de United States," Jeremiah said to Abraham.

"I can't believe it Jeremiah. I can't believe what I heard. The president, President Lincoln has been shot. Who kilt the president Jeremiah?" Abraham asked.

"Lieutenant White, sir, who was it that shot the president?" Abraham asked.

"A rebel sympathizer private Jackson did the shooting. That is, a man who supported the South, who believed in the Southern cause. War is not easy. It is inhuman and barbaric. Private, death is something that every soldier faces and lives with. That'll be all private Jackson."

Lieutenant White reminded the men of the good deeds of President Lincoln. It was President Abraham Lincoln who issued the Emancipation Proclamation that freed them from bondage. This new freedom gave them a chance to choose how they would live their lives. Abraham and Jeremiah were late in enlisting in the union army. It was the stroke of President Lincoln's pen that gave them a chance to fight for, and preserve their freedom.

Abraham reflected on the conversation he'd heard from his former slave boss and others about the fate of the war. It was true, he thought to himself. The war effort had gone badly for the confederacy. General Sherman and his armies had scurried across Georgia destroying plantations and the personal property of the southern slaveholders. It was true about southern defeat in Darien two years earlier and off the coast of Georgia near Brunswick and St. Simons Island.

In June the Thirty-Third received orders to report to Augusta, Georgia. They left Savannah on June 9, 1865 and marched into Augusta in record time, arriving six days later. After their two week stay in Augusta they moved to Hamburg South Carolina in July for provost and guard duty. The Thirty-Third Regiment stayed in Savannah three months before leaving for Augusta in June 1865.

Abraham and the men of his Company celebrated the Fourth of July outside of the town of Hamburg, South Carolina. They sang and danced and enjoyed Independence Day. They celebrated America's eighty-ninth year of Independence from England. Abraham's celebration was hampered by the thought that he missed his wife and children. He longed to return to see them as he contemplated where the Thirty-Third's next assignment would take him. He thought of the long march from Savannah to Augusta. He recalled that Savannah was a large place and it seemed to him as if a million colored troops were stationed there when he first arrived in March. He was proud to be a part of what he called Abe Lincoln's Army.

Later Abraham stopped daydreaming and joined the other soldiers in celebrating Independence Day. Before they ate their special meal for the day, they enjoyed singing, dancing, and foot racing. The officers of Company C enjoyed the day with the men of the Thirty-Third helping them to commemorate Independence Day and enjoy the festivities of the afternoon.

"Come on Abram, sing us a song," shouted one of the men. "Put aside your Bible and sing us a song," he hollered out.

Abraham interrupted: "Here we are Jeremiah, sing us a song, I'se too tired from running against those fast moving human rabbits. I am too tired to sing."

Three hours later the Independence Day celebration came to an end; the soldiers ate the food and drink the holiday beverage that was prepared for them. This was the first day Abraham and the men celebrated their freedom from slavery and America's independence from England simultaneously. The fun and merrymaking came to an end, but the soldiers were still engaged in horse play and laughter.

"Here we is Abraham: Singing, laughing, dancing, and playing around. But we still ain't free."

"What do you mean Joseph? Abraham interrupted."

"I can't explain it, but I seed how the white folk look at us when we marched into Augusta. They look at us like we was some kind of animal; like a weasel in a chicken house, or a dog with fleas all over his back and can't scratch."

"You is right Joseph. Jeremiah noted, the same thing happened to me a short time ago. The colored soldiers have been in this war since Abe Lincoln set us free. But those buckra ain't used to seeing nigger soldiers with rifles controlling the streets. Remember you is a slave boy, not a Massa," Abraham jokingly laughed.

"One day us will be free jest like de buckra soldiers. Our chilun" and grand chilun' will laugh 'bout it; us have de good Lawd on our side." Joseph grinned.

Time passed quickly, five months later on December 18, 1865 the Congress of the United States passed the Thirteenth Amendment to the United Constitution freeing all slaves in the United States including the Border States. The amendment declared "Neither slavery nor involuntary servitude, except as a punishment for crime whereof the party shall have been duly convicted, shall exist within the United States, or any place subject to their jurisdiction."

The Thirteenth Amendment went far beyond the Emancipation Proclamation which freed the slaves in the states that rebelled against the United States government. The Emancipation Proclamation didn't free a single slave in the loyal Border States. The news of the passage of the Thirteenth Amendment was a joyous time for all African Americans in the United States. Slavery had been a legal institution in the United States for more than two centuries.

Every free moment Abraham received he read the Bible that was given to him by the Company chaplain. He also read his blue back spelling book every chance he got. In slavery he'd been denied the right to learn to read and write. He was anxious to learn to read; now he could write and spell his name. He was learning how to do simple arithmetic. Some of the older soldiers who'd enlisted earlier in the war were writing letters to their families. Abraham was entertaining the idea of learning to write a letter before being mustered out of the army.

The freedmen and women in Charleston welcomed the presence of African American soldiers in the area. The ebony soldiers represented a sign of hope and protection for African Americans in the area. The end of the war had left both African American and their former slave masters destitute. Many former slaves moved from area to area and town to town in search of work and the bare necessities of life.

Chapter Twelve

The Thirty-Third Regiment marched into Fort Wagner the sight of a fierce bloody battle two years earlier between Union and rebel forces. The famous Fifty-Fourth Massachusetts Volunteers led the charge for control of the fort beginning on July 18, 1863. Abraham began to think about the horrors of war as they entered the area where three weeks of gruesome fighting occurred. Here at Battery Wagner hundreds of men were killed and many more were wounded. The smell of sea water penetrated his nostrils and he could taste the salty water from the ocean. He could hear the thunder of the big guns as shells exploded on impact as men fell all around and over each other.

Abraham thought about death and dying. What price must men pay for freedom, yet the black man wasn't fully free. Why would one volunteer his services to fight for a cause and leave his family in a hostile land? He asked himself: Was the sacrifice worth it? He could feel the sand flying into the eyes of the young soldiers; shells exploding and bursting all around them. The deafening screams of the men, the waves from the ocean pushing bodies to the edge of the sea. Seconds later, Abraham snapped out of his deep thought as he came to grips with himself and the purpose of the war.

The second week in January he sustained an injury to his left shoulder while helping to load a gun carriage. He and Jeremiah and four other men with him slipped and all of the weight fell on Abraham damaging his shoulder and leg. He was taken to the army hospital on Sullivan's Island. He was treated daily by the army surgeon. His second day in the hospital he received a visit from his fellow soldier and friend Jeremiah.

"Private Jackson, how is you this morning? Jeremiah smiled. He saw the pain on Abraham's face as he showed discomfort from the shoulder injury.

"In pain my buddy what about you, how is you doing?"

"I had guard duty all night. What did the doctor say? How long will you be here?" Jeremiah asked.

"I can't move my left shoulder. I'se be here 'til I'm mustered out."

"What is you gwine to do when you is mustered out Abraham?"

"I'se going back to my wife and chilun'; learn to read and write; buy some land and find my mother and brothers if dey is still alive." It was painful for Abraham to talk as he frowned and touched his left shoulder with his right hand.

"What about you, Jeremiah. What is you going to do?"

"I don't know yet. I'se going to follow the North Star; wherever it leads me I will go. I do not know, if my papa is dead or alive. He was sold away from my sisters and me."

"When I leave the army I'm going to get me forty horses and an acre of land." Abraham laughed clinching his teeth as Jeremiah spoke. The doctor interrupted Abraham and Jeremiah's conversation as he walked in to examine his shoulder. He had Abraham to sit up and removed the bandage from his injured shoulder. He pressed against Abraham's shoulder, first, pushing lightly and then more forceful to gauge the level of pain in his shoulder. He placed a new bandage around his shoulder, and nodded his head in approval at the progress Abraham was making.

"Are you feeling better private?" The doctor asked. Do you have a headache or any fever?" He asked as he touched Abraham's forehead. He gave him a pill to ease the pain and help him to rest better.

"You mean you want to get forty acres and a horse. I know you was joking about getting forty horses and a acre of land. I would be glad to get three horses and two mules. I'll find a way to get the land. I just want this shoulder to heal," Abraham said easing his body to the bed. Anyway, Jeremiah you meant to say forty acres and a mule, not a horse.

Two weeks later Abraham was released from the hospital and returned to his regular duties at the fort. He felt much better as his shoulder began to heal and he was able to march with the other soldiers and perform his duties with little discomfort. He was happy and upbeat and felt better as the days passed by. He followed the doctor's instructions and didn't lift any heavy objects that would aggravate his injury.

On January 31, 1866 the men of the Thirty-Third received orders to be mustered out of the Union army. Abraham had enlisted at Savannah for three years. The men cheered and were overjoyed at the good news. It was a cold windy day at Fort Wagner as Captain White spoke to the men in his company about their discharge. Lieutenant White was promoted to captain in September 1865. He wished them the best of luck as they returned to civilian life; and it was his wish that they enjoyed their new found freedom. He reminded them to apply the skills they'd learned in the army when they returned to their former residences. He cautioned them they were no longer the slaves of their former masters. They were the masters of their own destiny. Being free means acquiring new habits and adjusting to new ways of thinking the captain summoned them.

As the men boarded the train that took them to their destinations Abraham thought to himself as he so often meditated and reflected on his past and future. He recognized that life in bondage had it boundaries which no slave could go beyond. He contemplated that life in freedom was no illusion and he must come face to face with reality, if he was ever going to experience real freedom. This freedom and happiness captured his imagination. Would he have to live with the memory of a terrifying and shameful past? Yesterday is gone, he theorized, but the memories of the past must not leave him bitter or angry. His identity as a slave must not contradict his character as a free person.

As the train moved closer toward Abraham's destination he continued to engross himself in deep thought about the sectional division of the nation and the problems of slavery and freedom. Four years of bitter fighting had resulted in the loss of thousands of lives and many more thousand were maimed or wounded. He thought to himself as he looked outside at the landscape. Tall pines waving against a strong February wind; he thought it was contemptible for the nation to be divided along sectional and racial lines. Four years of bitter fighting in which the wounds of war would soon heal, but the scars of sectionalism and racism would remain for generations.

Thirty minutes later the train pulled into the station as it arrived at its destination. When he stepped from the train he was surprised to see that soldiers in blue surrounded the area. The entire county was under military control. Abraham contemplated on returning to civilian life as a farmer. The occupation he was engaged in before his enlistment. The idea of receiving forty acres and a mule ran through his mind. It was his dream to acquire more land after he settled down. He thought of Rilla and his four children and how they were doing.

The South had to go through a process of rebuilding. He knew before he was mustered out that the Southern states were under military control. While in Augusta, Aiken, Hamburg, and Charleston he was a part of the military occupation forces. He thought how Reconstruction in Georgia would affect him and the former slaves in the area. Thanks to the good Lord that we whipped old Jeff Davis and the Confederacy, he smiled to himself touching his hat with his right hand.

Abraham kept looking ahead to see if he could locate Rilla and their small children. Half frozen and weather beaten from the frigid cold of winter; he continued to march as he moved closer to the former slave cabins. Water streamed down his face as the icy wind blew against his body. Suddenly he spotted Rilla who was about to walk inside the cabin. No other faces could be seen on the outside because of the bitter cold. As he moved closer she recognized him. She ran over to where he stood; Abraham dropped his army bag to the ground as they embraced each other. "Chilun' yo pa is back," Rilla screamed out. Everyone was hypnotized with excitement and happy to see him.

Chapter Thirteen

Two hours later Abraham arrived where he'd left eleven months earlier. The entire family was overcome with joy as they saw him dressed in his blue Union army uniform. Rilla, George, Harriet, Macy Ann, and Lewis were delighted to see their father as he entered the small cabin he'd left eleven months earlier. He threw his army bag aside and gave everyone a big hug.

"You children show have growed, look at George. He is almost as tall as me," Abraham said placing his hand on the top of George's head. "Harriet and Macy you girls have growed a lot too. Little Lewis, how old is you?" Abraham roared lifting him above his head. "I missed you little children so much. I thought of you every day when I was away."

Rilla observed something different about Abraham. He sounded different in his speech and in his demeanor. She thought to herself, he doesn't talk as he did before he joined Abe Lincoln's Army. Maybe they changed him, but he was only gone for eleven months. He has to teach us how to talk like him.

"Dere was sojers all around us when you were gone. Dey wore blue. De other sojers I was told had gray uniforms. Dey were Abe Lincoln's sojers, that was what us heard. Us didn't see old Massa or Miss Sarah for a long time. I'se heard de sojers ran them away," Rilla said laughing. We heard so many tings dat happened. When I heard dat President Lincoln was kilt, we thought dey said Abraham Jackson. We was so scarid."

Later that night the children were asleep Abraham and Rilla talked about things that happened when he was away. Rilla was so glad to know that he had come back safely.

"Thanks the Lord the fighting is over," Abraham said in a sincere voice. We whipped old Jeff Davis and his rebels." Abraham smiled. When the news came to us that the war was over I was in Savannah. Then a week later, the news came to us that president Lincoln had been assassinated, that is he had been shot and killed."

Again Rilla noticed a difference in the way her husband spoke. Before he left he talked like the other former slaves and the colored people in the area. She wanted to speak like her husband. She could hardly find the words to ask him why he spoke differently. She concluded that he was taught while he was in the army. He must have learned quickly she surmised.

"Abram, you don' talk like you did 'befo you joined Abe Lincoln's Army. Now you talk like dem other folks. Dat's good. I will learn to talk like you one day Abraham Jackson." She shrugged.

"Rilla, now that we are free we can be taught to speak correctly. One day we can have our own school and teachers to teach. In the large cities they have the Freedmen's Bureau. When I was in Charleston they had schools and teachers to teach the colored children. That's my dream to see that the colored children and anyone else who can't read and write to be taught." Abraham asserted.

"Abram, while you was away George and Harriet got sick wid de feber. De old herb doctor told me to rub something on dey necks dat smelt and looked like turpentine. Dey didn't like it. Dat stuff smelt awful. He told me to walk backward 'round de house seven times. Den he told me to put seven drops in my tracks. I'se don' dat and two days later dey was running and playing. It seemed so silly what he said."

The next morning Abraham was out of bed at daybreak. Arising early ahead of time was no problem for him. During slavery he was up at daybreak to prepare for that day's task by sunup. During his eleven month stay in the Union army every soldier had to awaken early for reveille. He had to return to his accustomed routine before he enlisted in the army.

After breakfast and all the children were awake; Abraham reminded George since he was the oldest child much more would be required of him. He had to take the lead in helping him and his mother do the required work around their house. George was energetic and eager to do whatever task was assigned him. He was taught early that he must always help take care of his younger brothers and sisters. He turned seven his last birthday and could do the work of a twelve—year old.

Later that morning after breakfast, and before Abraham talked to his former slave master he was anxious to show Rilla what he'd done ten days before Christmas. He was proud of what he was going to show and tell her. He reached for his bag where he had the surprise waiting for her. "Here it is," he grinned holding up a piece of paper. "I tried to write you a letter before Christmas, but I never finished it."

"It wid not hab did any good; because I doesn't know how to read. I'se didn't know you know how to read and write. You must've learnt in Abe Lincoln's army."

Abraham grinned as he showed Rilla a blank piece of paper he'd kept since December of 1865. "I just wanted to see how you looked when you saw the paper. "I know how to write and spell my name. I know how to count a little bit. I learned how to read and just a little bit. I can read a few words from the Bible, but that's all a few words. And I can talk a little better than when I first left."

"I'se got to tell this Abram, 'befo you goes and talk wid Massa Collins, if you see him."

"What do you mean, if I see him."

"Abe old Massa thought he was gwine to die. He called fer us to come and sing to him. He kept saying: Sing dat song 'chilun, dat you sang in de fields. I likes dat song and us hadn't sang anyting yet. He thought I was Alice. We singed one song—Gwine to see de good Lawd when I die.

"Lawd, Alice gives Massa Collins some rabbit 'bacco tea and put some turpentine in it and had him to drink it hot. Dat mess was so bitter old Massa almos' spit it up. De next day he was almost his usual self; he was jest cussin' and hollerin' at every one. He was as happy as a fox in a chicken coop."

Abraham thought it was funny how scared old Massa was. He knew that things would be better for him and his family because the federal troops were located in the area. They were stationed at the courthouse. He talked to his former slave boss and the two of them agreed that Abraham could continue to work the plot of land he did before his enlistment. It was mid February and Abraham had to get the farm animal he had before he left and farm tools and become re-employed at his old job. He saw Frank and Henry who seemed to have grown at least three inched taller since he left. He would soon be ready to get started farming as before he left. His left shoulder still aggravated him whenever he lifted objects over fifty pounds. He could still feel a sharp pain.

Later that night Abraham had settled in and was back to his normal routine. He had found everyone in good health and energetic. His former slave boss appeared more considerate than before he left. The temperature had begun to drop as the cold wind increased in velocity. It blew from the Northwest onto the small cabin.

"Next month I'll start breaking ground for planting." Abraham disclosed to Rilla. "I'll have to get some seed. First, I need to get all my farm tools and supplies lined up; then I'll plant corn seed first, and then cotton seed later. After I've worked a few months, I want to buy me a tract of land to farm for myself."

"Where is you gwine to get money to buy land for a farm?"

"I saved a few dollars while I was in Abe Lincoln's army. I will work with old man Collins and save a few dollars more. Soon Rilla we will have our own land and farm."

"I heard after you left that colored people would get forty acres and a mule. I heard Henry say that and he heard it from old Massa Collins. Dey was talking about it."

"I heard that too Rilla, but that's about it. That Bureau that was set up last year to help us colored people was talking about helping us who was former slaves. But whether we get forty acres and a mule or not, I is going to save enough money to buy my own farm."

Time passed quickly as Abraham and Rilla talked until the light from the lamp grew dim. An hour later they had finished talking and were in bed. Soon the wood in the heater had burned down and the heat soon exited the room. The temperature continued to drop throughout the night as the cabin grew cooler from the frigid February weather.

Early the next morning Abraham had the cabin warm as the outside temperature gradually began to warm up. All the children had arisen as the excitement of their father's return made them cheerful and animated. Abraham heard a knock on the cabin door. "Come in Henry, come on in." Henry entered with a surprised look on his face. "How did you know it was me? I didn't tell you I was coming. He reached out to shake Abraham's hand, "how is you doing, I hasn't seed you since you left to join Abe Lincoln's army. As I think 'bout it I didn't see you 'befo you left."

"I'd know that knock anywhere Henry." I am just common Henry. Rilla told me last night that you'd be coming over here this morning. I see you didn't freeze; the weather is cold outside."

"I have a surprise for you Abraham; I been savin' it for six months. Don't look. I'll get it for you. I'se didn't know where you was dead or alive wid de war going on, and all."

"As you can see Henry I am alive and well, except for a few aches and pains. What have you been doing for yourself? Are you farming now? I hadn't heard anything from you."

"Well, Abraham, here is 'yo surprise." Henry kept smiling and moving backwards. "Every since you left, I'se been telling Rilla and Sally, I'se gwine to surprise you if you got back."

Abraham wondered to himself what Henry was talking about. What kind of surprise he had for him. He couldn't think of what Henry may've had for him. If Rilla knew, she didn't tell him. "Okay Henry, I can't figure it out. I'm afraid you'll have to tell me."

"Here is the jug I'se been telling you 'bout." Abraham wondered what was inside the jug as he uncorked the top. He was startled as well as overwhelmed. "Henry, that smells like apple cider." Rilla gave him a glass to pour the liquid substance into the chalice what he thought was apple cider. "That looks like wine, Henry," Abraham said as he tasted the contents in the glass. It tastes good Henry, and you've had it about six months. It smells like apple cider and tastes like wine." Abraham chuckled.

"Betta be careful now Abraham, don't let it knock you off 'yo foots." Henry said as he looked at Rilla and Sally in a burst of laughter. "That ting will knock you out and you won't be able to do any work dis moanin.' I 'sho is glad you is back Abraham. Abe Lincoln's sojers is all over dis area. Dey is all in de courthouse."

The day began to gradually warm up. Abraham, Frank, Henry, and George left early for work to cut down trees for Mr. Collins. Abraham was working on shares with his former Massa and working his acre of land; his former Massa agreed to parcel him off another acre of land. Abraham was thrilled to receive the extra acre of land to add to the five he already had. He would plant his acre in cotton or corn and equally divide it with Massa Collins. He continued to reflect upon the idea of having his own farm. He knew he would have to work hard each day. He was forewarned in a dream that the weather would be favorable for the planting of his crops and old man Collins crops. He wasn't the only one working for his former slave Massa. Henry, Charlie and Isaac, were working the land on shares, but didn't want the responsibility of having their own land and working it.

Later in the afternoon Rilla was washing clothes on the side of the cabin. The children were playing hide and seek around her and moving from side to side. The afternoon temperature was cool and the smell of wood burning in the air and clothes boiling in lye soap could be detected a mile away. Abraham and Rilla's two brothers, Frank and Henry and seven year old George worked hard all day clearing land. Time passed quickly, and the work day soon came to an end. Abraham continued to reflect and deliberate on what needed to be done if he and the African Americans fresh out of slavery were to be become successful and overcome ignorance and illiteracy. The first thing that was needed was for his people to learn to read and write. Education was the best safeguard that could be used to overcome illiteracy, he thought.

The next day Charlie and Sallie came around to greet Abraham and celebrate his return home. It was a Saturday afternoon and everyone was in a festive mood. Abraham's return brightened the day for all who knew him. He saw Charlie out the corner of his eyes as he motioned for the children to go outside and play. Excited about seeing his friend, Abraham rushed over to shake Charlie's hand.

Charlie sprang to his feet and greeted Abraham with a handshake. "How is you doing? I is so glad to see you. I haven' saw you in coon days. Charlie's voice trembled as he spoke: "I'se so happy and glad to see that you is back from de war. Sallie and us didn't know how you was. De late war hab' dis state under de control of Abe Lincoln's army. Dere is sojers everywhere us goes. Old Massa Collins is still 'scarid of de sojers. One ting I is still waiting for Abraham, and dat is my forty acres and a mule. I doesn't hear no talk 'bout dat anymore. I'd be glad if I had forty mules and an acre." Charlie joked.

"My friend Jeremiah joked about having forty horses and an acre of land. That's what General Sherman said after he arrived in Savannah. But that was in the Savannah area. That won't help us poor folk a lot who are trying to farm.

"We have to be patient Charlie. Some good things will happen for us soon. I have been telling everyone since I got back, that we need to learn to read and write. That's all I can think of. It will help us and our children to progress; we've got to teach our children" Abraham explained.

"I knowed Abraham, since you is been back you is gwine to help us to learn to read and write. I wants to learn to read de Bible, dat's all I wants to do. But us can't let old Massa Collins and de other buckra folk hear us talking like dis. I had sometin' for you boy, but Sallie broke it 'befo I gets a chance to give it to you."

"Seeing you Charlie, that's all the present I want."

"You listen to Abraham, Charlie, he can talk better now. He ain't gwine to let old Massa Collins cheat us. He knows what to say and when to say it. "I is proud of my son-in-law." My two boys Frank and Henry, they love to be wid him and work wid him. You listen to him and learn something."

"You should've saw Massa running Abraham. He was trying to hide from Abe Lincoln's sojers. Dem sojers took fifteen of old Massa's cows. Dey kilt all of dem and several of his hogs and chickens. Dat was the last sojers I saw." Charlie roared with laughter. "It was de middle of May 'befo us knowed de war was over."

In early March the United States Congress passed the Civil Rights Act of 1866 which provided freedom for the former slaves and the protection of their rights which were denied to them in slavery. The Act provided that the freedmen could enter into contracts and make contracts and not be cheated out of their rightful labor. The Act was welcome news for Abraham. Now he could see some of the things come to fruition which he'd dreamed of.

Chapter Fourteen

A year later the United States Congress passed the Reconstruction Act of 1867. Reconstruction was a time of restoration and reconciliation. The transition from slavery to freedom was a difficult process for the former slaves and their owners who'd enslaved them. It was a time for the former bondsmen to attain political, social, and economic rights enjoyed by all Americans. The Reconstruction Act of March 1867 provided African Americans the opportunity to register and vote for the first time since they were freed by the Thirteenth Amendment to the United States Constitution in December of 1865.

Luke was excited about his newfound political rights and was eager to participate in the political process; he greeted Abraham with exuberance. "Abraham, the next thing we need to do is to learn to read and write. Ain't like it was when us was in slavery. Us is free now, Mr. Abraham," Luke smiled. "Us ain't gwine to work no more for free; us is free, de good Lawd don' heard our prayers."

"Yes, Luke, it's good to have freedom and enjoy it. If we are going to stay free, we have got to learn to read and write. When we do this, we can keep our freedom." Abraham admonished Luke.

Minutes later, Abraham saw Charlie and Sampson and greeted them. Federal troops were still stationed all around the wooden building to protect the former slaves as they registered to vote for the first in their lives. "Charlie, you and Sampson came here to sign up. Now Sampson, don't let anyone cut your hair before you register." Abraham chuckled. "We don't want you to lose your strength and become an ordinary man like me."

"Yes sir, Mr. Abe, Sampson and I is gwine to register today, Us is gwine to put our x on de place by our names." Charlie grinned. "Today, us is gwine to become voters in dis county."

"It's a trick Charlie," James exclaimed, looking at Abraham and Luke. He spoke in a low voice not wanting anyone to hear him except for Abraham and Luke. "Luke, you is older than dem young ones. "I can't reed or wite, but I doesn't want to be put back in bondage. Mr. Joe said dem Yankee sojers is tying to trick us. If us place an x on dat line by our names old Massa can put us back in slavery." James spoke in an almost inaudible voice.

"That's not true James." Abraham pleaded. Colored people are free now. And we have a right to register and vote just like anyone else. I don't know everything, but I can read and write a little. And nowhere on that paper, does it say, if we register the old slave Massa will take away our freedom."

"Naw, James, Luke growled in a high pitched voice. "Us is free now, Mr. President Lincoln signed dat 'Mancipation Prock'lamason four years ago and made us free people. De war is over, de Souse lost and us niggers is gwine to vote now."

An hour later, many African Americans, former slaves that were made illiterate by the state slave code of Georgia; had registered to vote under the protection of federal soldiers that were stationed inside and outside of the county courthouse. This day marked an important date in the life of many African American men since the county was created sixty-six years earlier.

Later that day just before Abraham left the county seat, he met his friend Jacob; who ran to greet Abraham, full of laughter and excitement. Abraham climbed from his wagon as Jacob grabbed the reins of his mule.

"Good evening, Abe. How is you doing dis evening? I ain't seed you in 'bout three weeks. I doesn't think I seed you since you were mustered out."

"Just common, Jake, how is you doing now?

"Great! I'm doing just great. I have already been here. I had to leave about three hours ago, but I'se back now. How is dat shoulder of yours? Is it still giving you trouble? "Jake sighed.

"Abe, did you know dat old Hiram is working wid de colored people, yeah he is talking to them so dey won't get scared and think their old slave boss will put em' back in slavery. Did you see Hiram dis morning? Yeah, he was dere standing tall; checking to make sho' de colored men registered to vote."

"Jacob, I heard that your commanding general is running for president in the upcoming election next year. I almost got a chance to see him before I was mustered out. Captain White said he came to Charleston about three weeks before we left."

"Abraham, did you hear me earlier? How is your left shoulder?"

"My shoulder is fine, until I lift something to heavy; when that happens I can tell. Then again, it bothers me when the weather gets cloudy and it's about to rain. I have to keep working Jake; I can't let a little pain stop me from going. I'll slow down when I get old."

In 1868 the United States Congress added the Fourteenth Amendment to the United States Constitution. This amendment made United States citizens of the former slaves. This was a requirement Georgia had to meet before it was readmitted to the Union. The Thirteenth Amendment abolished slavery and now the fourteenth Amendment granted the former slaves national citizenship rights. Abraham and the African American citizens in Georgia and Tattnall County were jubilant about the passage of the new amendment.

African Americans were people with the same needs and desires as other United States citizens. They were no longer the property of slave owners, but free people; entitled to the same privileges and immunities as other U.S. citizens. Abraham and other African American men desired to proclaim and exercise their citizenship rights through the power of the elective franchise. African American voters in Georgia voted to send black men to the Georgia general assembly for the first time under the Reconstruction Act that had empowered them with the ballot. Tunis G. Campbell who represented Liberty, McIntosh, and Tattnall Counties became a member of the Georgia senate.

Abraham, Jacob, and the African American men of Tattnall County became enraged with anger when they learned Georgia had expelled its Black leaders in July of the same year. After widespread protest of white radical Republicans and newly elected blacks in the United States House of Representative they regained their seats.

"Well Jacob, I thought our problem ended when Lee laid down his arms to Grant at Appomattox courthouse in old Virginny. We ain't soldiers anymore, but we still have problems. Now, look at this, Jacob. The Fourteenth Amendment said we is United States citizens and the Fifteenth Amendment just passed says we have the right to vote. But we are still struggling."

"Can we call it a victory for Georgia and the South? Abram, can we call it a victory for the colored man? They done passed all of these laws to free us, make us United States citizens, grant us the right to vote, us have made a little progress, but not much." Jacob lamented.

African Americans in Georgia faced a formidable task in keeping and enjoying their new found freedom. A terrorist group, the Ku Klux Klan used scare tactics to frighten the newly freed slaves. Many former slaves who attempted to exercise their political right to vote were attacked and beaten.

Abraham quickly recognized that the struggle to attain full freedom was a difficult process. The broken promises and the setbacks were a test of his ability to survive during this difficult time in Georgia's history. He felt that African Americans had to move forward and persevere; and look to a higher authority as they did while in bondage; if their freedom were to be everlasting. The former slaves and the former slave bosses needed each other. The former plantation owners and farmers needed the former slaves to work the land and the former slaves needed the land for work and survival.

Abraham, Aberdeen, Luke, Loance, and Jacob met the following week to discuss the priorities that were needed in order of time for them to move forward. The men recognized the terror and brutality faced by African Americans. The presence of federal soldiers helped to deter conspicuous violence in the county. But they recognized their greatest shortcoming.

"We need to learn to read and write. The best weapon the white folks have against us is our own ignorance. Until we can fight back, not with our fists or guns, but with knowledge, we will always be slaves to them." Abraham complained.

"And another thing," Loance reminded the group. "Us has got to have our own land. Lots of coloreds is leaving the county and going to the North. I can understand that, they is afraid of being beat up and kilt by the buckra and those paddy rollers."

"I heard two buckra men talking de other day. They said they'd be glad when President Abe Lincoln's Army left this county. Yes, I heard them say, de black nigger Republicans gwine to take over de state."

The Georgia legislature had already voted to kick its African American representatives and senators out of office. Turmoil continued to exist throughout the state as Georgia fought to gain readmission into the union. Night riders continued to terrorize African American voters whipping and killing suspected voters.

The courageous trio of Abraham, Loance, and Luke were overjoyed at voting in the presidential election of 1868. In November of that year, African Americans voted in their first presidential election as a free people. This was their first experience as a free people since the beginning of the Republic. Rejoicing took place throughout the small rural county. The new voters were escorted inside the courthouse by federal troops to cast their ballot for Ulysses S. Grant, the Republican presidential candidate. The morning was cold and dreary as Abraham made the five mile trek to the courthouse.

"Abraham us can vote now. De good Lawd has heard our prayers. I is so glad that we is free men and not the property of buckra men anymore."

"I neber did tink dat I'd see dis day." Luke shouted out."

"Yessuh, us is got to keep on praying to de good Lawd. I is fifty years old. I'd been de property of Massa Eason since I was born. And last year was de first time I was able to vote. Loance grinned.

"The Thirteenth Amendment made us free. President Abraham Lincoln's 'Emancipation Proclamation freed us too. De good Lawd has bressed us all." Luke roared.

The next day Tom spoke to Abraham about a horrible incident that happened just two days earlier. He'd taken a group of men to the polls in an adjoining county. And the man's place he was living on warned him not to vote if he did he'd be whipped and possibly lynched.

"Yes, they whipped my cousin; then came to my house; knocked on the door and busted it down. Dragged me out into the road, told me to get up and knocked me down again. And then hit me several times across the head. Later they dragged me into the woods and tied me to a black gum tree."

"Dey placed a rope around my neck and said, Abe Lincoln got what he deserved, a bullet through his head. He should've never set the niggers free. Then he said nigger! Let this be a lesson to you; don't get involved in white peoples politics."

Having listened to this story Abraham became furious and unhappy. He had difficulty composing himself. He was speechless for close to an hour. He began to meditate and think of the violence he'd seen during slavery and while he was on guard and provost duty in the towns and cities where he was stationed with the Thirty-Third Regiment. Why did the colored man have to suffer so much to attain and keep his freedom? Nothing, he thought would keep him from exercising his rights as a free person. And the right to vote for the people of his choice was one way to exercise that right. He found it difficult to contain his emotions as he thought of how innocent colored men were attacked by mobs of whites who intimidated them physically and used the threat of economic coercion to keep them in fear of exercising their constitutional right to vote.

Following his talk with Tom, an hour later Abraham was back working clearing another acre of his five acres he'd received from his former slave owner. George was now ten years of age and was of profitable help to Abraham in helping clear his land. While Abraham, Frank, and Henry dug the roots and stomps from the ground, George helped to carry them off. He was helped by his younger six-year old brother, Lewis. Abraham and his work crew hammered the difficult trees, stumps, and roots extricating them from the soil. They worked long and hard for the remainder of the day until an hour before dusk dark. They worked at three hour intervals and rested for thirty minutes and then returned to work on clearing the land.

Later that evening, before dark, Abraham reflected on what work he had done earlier in the day. He was pleased at the work and pace he and Rilla's brothers and two smaller children were doing. He began talking out loud to himself as he walked to the rear of the cabin.

"Rilla, I am pleased with the five acres of land that we have. Old Massa Collins has had a change of heart; but I want more than five acres of land. I want some land I can have freely by myself with no former slave boss telling me what and when to plant and not to plant."

"We work the land from sun to sun. It is like walking up a hill and never reaching the top. I am going to work and have something. Abe, I think you are doing well," Abraham thought to himself. Little George and Lewis enjoy working wid you. The girls are getting bigger. They are growing every day. Little Abraham is three years old and even he wants to work."

"I have been looking at some land about six miles from here. It's close to three miles from that river with that funny name. I can't buy it now, because I don't have enough money. I heard the man wants twenty-five cents an acre."

"Abraham who was you talking too? I heard you talking out loud. Rilla asked.

"No one Rilla, I was just talking to myself."

Early the next day Abraham became so busy thinking about clearing his other acres of land for planting he'd almost forgotten that Georgia was still under military rule. Three years had passed since he'd left the military and he was eager to return to his former occupation, but as a free man. He continued to meditate about the plight of the African American in his struggle to overcome racial injustice and be treated fairly and equally as any other American citizen. He was anxious to find out how his other former slave companions were doing. He knew and recognized the issues that confronted him and them.

It was a warm March day. It felt like spring as he drove his wagon to John Rivers place. The birds sang as they flew overhead and landed in a tall pine tree. Abraham's red shirt and his blue coat with his left pocket torn was a perfect contrast. The old wagon squeaked as he rolled over sinking holes in the road. He saw eight men working in the field cutting logs and removing stomps from the earth. This was a reminder of the work he did on yesterday. Abraham yelled for the stubborn mule to stop as he and the cumbersome four-wheeled vehicle came to a halt. Abraham was cheerful and nothing could dampen his spirit.

Chapter Fifteen

The year was 1875 and Abraham and Rilla had ten children. Four were born since his return from the Civil War. Amanda was born in 1868; Nancy in 1870; Benjamin in 1872, and Andrew in 1874. Abraham knew, now was his chance to move forward. He thought, when this day is past, I'll never see it again. He continued in deep thought. I am no longer human chattel, or what the nation had rendered me, three-fifths of a man; he concluded to himself.

The years passed swiftly and Abraham found himself talking to a man who had land for sale. He'd been thinking for years about buying a good tract of farmland and timber. He worked inexhaustible for days and months to purchase land. He'd saved fifty dollars through his tireless effort and hard work to go along with the money he saved while in the army during the Civil War.

"I tell you what uncle Abram if you and your boys would be willing to help me cut the trees from some of the land, I'll sell it to you for twenty-five cents an acre. How does that sound uncle?"

"I want to purchase three-hundred acres. Abraham said. My boys and I can do that. And you is going to sell me three-hundred acres at twenty-five cents per acre."

"I tell you what uncle Abram, if you and your boys and whoever else you get to help cut the trees from the land, it's a deal.

When the rains come this winter we can float the logs down the Ohoopee into the Altamaha and on to the market at Darien."

Abraham was happy to hear the good news. He thought Mr. Wade was going to ask him to pay fifty cents an acre.

"It's a deal Mr. Wade. As soon as I finish my crops we'll get started."

"I've been watching you uncle; you ain't like most of the nigras, I mean colored people around here. I saw you at the courthouse a few months ago."

"Well, Mr. Wade, I'm just a common man. I want to be treated like any other man. I want what is fair for me and my family."

"You will be getting a fine tract of land. You know this land was once owned by the Creek Indians. They were on this land before the people from Spain came here. They were a group of savages and didn't know what to do with the land. They lived by the creeks and rivers, that's how they got the name Creek. They did nothing but hunt and fish; they lived a simple life. Did you know that uncle Abram?"

"I'm just a simple colored man myself. I don't know much about Indians; just wants to farm and raise my children to respect others, and treat them the way that they wish to be treated."

"You know uncle some of my people ain't going to like it, me selling you this land and all. But you are helping pay for it by grubbing and cutting logs for me. Well, I'll be in touch with you."

The day passed quickly and Abraham had to take care of some unfinished business. He knew he'd made a step in the right direction and would be able to benefit from the plan he and Mr. Wade had worked out. He was elated. His children were getting older and growing. George was sixteen years of age; Lewis was fourteen; and Abraham Jr. was twelve years of age and growing. He could depend on Rilla's two brothers, Frank and Henry. Though they were grown men; Frank was twenty-five and Henry was twenty-two.

The federal troops were still stationed at the courthouse in Reidsville. The state was still a perilous place for African Americans. There was daily talk that the federal troops would soon leave the state. Abraham continued his hard work preparing to purchase his three-hundred acre tract of land. He talked to his friend Jacob and a young man called Israel who was seeing his second oldest daughter, Israel joined him in clearing his new tract of land.

Two months later in the latter part of November, Abraham and his sons traveled to his new tract of land. They had been working for four weeks clearing the land, cutting down trees and digging up stomps.

"Papa, I know there is lots of rabbits, squirrels, and raccoons, on this land." George laughed.

"What about deer, foxes, and bears," clamored Lewis. "Didn't you tell me you heard the sound of a big catamount, George?"

"Boys we is got to get our shovels, axes, and hoes, and whatever tools we can use to help us clear this land. Maybe we can get some of those bears and cats to help out." Abraham laughed growling as if he was a bear.

The vegetation on the land was plentiful. There were all kinds and varieties of tall pines, oaks, and black gum trees. Wild animals used the thick vegetation for protection. Rabbits leaped and scampered through the woods; squirrels were frightened as they jumped from tree to tree. A few wild turkeys were spotted flying and landing in the tall pines; then taking off in a burst of speed and sailing through the air. Several species of birds flew over the area and nested in the trees. Abraham's new land was a haven and refuge for many wild animals.

Before the end of the work day George mentioned to Abraham what he'd heard the past month about the land he was purchasing. Abraham listened intently at what was being said.

"I heard talk papa last month about a black bear walking near the river bank of that river with the funny name. I heard talk of a large catamount in the area too. A white man spotted one papa. Two white men said they seed one 'bout three miles from here."

"Don't worry about that son. I don't think we'll have to worry about big cats and bears. Let's hope that it's all talk." George's eyes stretched as he saw Abraham pull a forty-four colt revolver from his overall pocket. "This will take care of any wild bears or cats around here." Abraham fired two shots into the air.

"What was that?" Frank shouted. "It sounded like a gun. Who did the shooting?"

"It was nothing Uncle Frank. Papa was just scaring off a few bears and big cats. That's a large gun papa; I didn't know you had it. Lewis told me he thought he'd seed you wid one, but I didn't believe him."

An hour later, Abraham and his boys returned to their home. George and Lewis took care of the mule giving her fodder and hay for the evening. They continued to make progress in clearing the land; felling trees and clearing away limbs and debris. Abraham was pleased with the progress they made for the day. He wanted to be finished with the section of land he'd marked out. He wanted to make a little progress each day before planting season arrived.

Rilla and her older girls had prepared a tasty meal for Abraham and the children. They had rabbit, sweet potatoes, mustard greens, and molasses water. Abraham said grace over the food and afterwards they enjoyed the food that was prepared for them.

"That was some good rabbit meat, Rilla." Abraham said patting his stomach. That's the best I've had in a long time. All the food was good. And we thank the good Lord for all of it."

"This place is getting too little fer us, Abram." They is ten of us now and de chilun' is getting' bigger. Dey is growin' like green corn."

"It won't be long. And we'll be gone from old Massa Collins place. We is going to have our own place. We is doing a little work each day and we'll soon be finished. Frank and Henry are hard workers. Jacob is helping us and Israel is working with us as well. Talking about Israel, Mace when have you seen him last."

"I saw him 'bout an hour ago. He said he is going to see me when he works wid you again."

"I've got to go to the courthouse tomorrow in Reidsville. I heard some talk that Abe Lincoln's soldiers will soon be leaving. Mr. Wade told me that the new man running for president said that he is going to remove all of Abe Lincoln's soldiers from the south and the state of Georgia. It won't be good for the colored people if this happens."

The next morning Abraham was up early as was his routine since his return to civilian life. He wanted to arrive early at the courthouse and observe what was happening. He wanted to find out if the rumors he'd heard were true. The five mile trip by wagon took him around an hour if travel time was to his advantage. The idle talk he heard coming from Mr. Wade, who was suddenly concerned about the colored peoples' affairs worried Abraham. And the idea that African American men would soon be disenfranchised left him even more troubled. As he entered the courthouse Ike Davis saw him and began telling him his views on what was happening in the county. He expressed to him how African Americans who wanted to register and vote were treated.

"I ain't gwine to register to vote Abraham. Colored men is getting beat up and some kilt for trying to do dat. Ben Hall got his coat ripped off of him for just being with a group of colored men. This happened about ten feet from where I was standing. It happened in broad daylight. He jest did 'scape wid his life."

"Ike, no one told me anything about this. I know I ain't been around here and haven't talked to anyone lately. I've heard some things but colored men can vote now. Ike, we could vote since 1867. We have been United States citizens for eight years. And what about the Fifteenth Amendment that further gave us the right to vote."

"Abraham, I ain't knowed nuttin' 'bout dese laws. Anyway, I hears dat de sojers dat is here will be leaving soon. They don' care nuttin' 'bout us. When they leave, us is in trouble."

Aberdeen recognized Abraham, and they immediately struck a conversation about the voting problem. Aberdeen voted for the first time under the Reconstruction Act of 1867. Loance was there as well; he too voted under the Reconstruction Act of 1867 in the county.

"Abraham, whatever happened to the colored senator us had. Didn't they kick him out of office?" Aberdeen muttered. "I heard he represented McIntosh, Liberty, and Tattnall Counties." Israel interrupted.

"Young man, where did you come from? I thought you were working with George and Frank today."

"Mr. Jackson, I am interested in the direction that us colored people need to go. If we ain't careful we'll be back in slavery. Too many colored men I know want to stop; to give up and not fight for their rights. When will we have a colored senator again in this county?"

Abraham knew what was going on in the county he heard and talked to several people he knew. But he was unfamiliar with what Ike told him. He reflected on what Aberdeen, Loance, and Israel had said. He had many things that clattered his mind, but didn't want to lose sight of his priorities and what he wanted to accomplish. His number one goal was to become fully literate himself. He wanted to clear the land; buy more farm tools; purchase a horse and wagon; build him a larger house to accommodate his growing family; and build a school and church on his newly purchased land. This was his dream since his return to civilian life.

Before he returned home he rode by Mr. Wade's to examine his newly purchased land and to check and see what needed to be done and how to proceed as fast as possible. Abraham knew there would be times when the weather would prevent them from working. He arrived at Mr. Wade's an hour and fifteen minutes after he left the courthouse. The day was a beautiful autumn afternoon; the temperature was average for October. He heard Mr. Wade talking as he climbed from the wagon. Mr. Wade was a loquacious gentleman and knew the affairs of everyone in the county.

"Uncle, I heard lots of coloreds in the county are registering to vote." Mr. Wade uttered a sly grin on his face.

"Don't know, Mr. Wade. I've been busy clearing land and working with Mr. Collins. I don't get a chance to see many people, you know." Abraham wasn't the type to volunteer information. He thought that the buckra man would use what he said to his disadvantage if he talked too much. This had been his experience throughout his years in involuntary servitude and since freedom.

"Uncle, are you a registered voter in the county?" Mr. Wade asked Abraham, a cunning grin on his face.

"Don't have too much time for politics." Abraham said, avoiding a direct answer to Mr. Wade's question.

The verbose Mr. Wade continued as Abraham listened. "You people have been treated wrong Uncle Abram. Now is the time that the colored people, be given a chance to participate in the government of this state and nation. You people had a colored senator right here in this county. I remember it was back in sixty nine or seventy. He was good for the county. I think he helped a lot of you colored people." Abraham wondered how long Mr. Wade was going to talk uninterrupted. He had to go and do other things while it was still light. He listened intently as the garrlous Mr. Wade spoke. Abraham began to move slowly toward his wagon thinking Mr. Wade would soon run out of words. He climbed aboard his wagon and saluted the talkative gentleman with the mischievous smile on his face; Mr. Wade was still talking as Abraham drove off.

Later that evening Abraham returned to his small house. "Rilla, that old man I'm buying the land from, runs his mouth non-stop all the time. I was glad to get away from him. He reminds me of old Sunrise; talking about the Indians. He says the land that I'm buying was once owned by the Creek Indians. They got that name because they lived by the Creeks in Georgia. He kept calling me uncle. I didn't know I had a white nephew. Did you know it Rilla? Abraham laughed.

"Rilla I have been talking with Jacob, Andy, and Israel. They want to help us establish a colored militia unit here in Tattnall County. What do you think about that; a colored militia unit; here in the county.

"Abram, is you sure what your nephew talked about didn't rub off on you. You sho' is talkin' a lot today. I ain't heard you talk this much in a long time. What is a militia unit? Is it something' like the army you were in. I think de colored men should have their own army."

Chapter Sixteen

"Rilla I remember when I first thought about asking your hand in marriage. I was so scared I was trembling on the inside trying to find the nerve to ask you. Your mama thought that I was going to run away again. What a time. I think about that sometimes now."

"No, Abram. Mama didn't want them slave catchers to catch you and chop off your feet. We was afraid dey would do something worse than cut of your feet. Those ole paddy rollers and slave catchers' was some evil wicked men. We feared for your safety."

"Well Rilla, twenty years later we have ten chilun' and one on the way. The good Lord has blessed our marriage. George has a girlfriend and he is getting married soon. He didn't see me, but I heard him tell Lewis about how pretty she was. Well, I have talked too much. It's time for me to get to work."

Before Abraham's work day began he saw a strange man in a buggy riding toward him, a small bay horse pulling the buggy. The man wore a dark blue shirt and had on a large brown hat. As he drove closer Abraham recognized him; he had seen him at the courthouse.

"Hello uncle." The man spoke, with a serious but, calm expression on his face. His voice trembled as he mumbled." How are you today?"

"Just common, not much better than the weather." Abraham relented. Abraham wore a dark green cotton shirt, the left pocket slightly torn. His shirt matched his dark brown pants. He sensed something was wrong; he didn't usually have a visitor that early in the morning.

"I'm J.W. Eason, the county constable." The short thin man stepped down from his buggy, his large black hat fell to the ground. He stooped down to pick up his hat but the wind blew it near where Abraham stood. Abraham picked the hat up and gave it to the sheriff. "Thank you uncle, the wind is blowing a little strong today." He reached into his pocket and pulled out a letter. "Abraham, I've been directed by the tax office to sell your land in front of the courthouse to the highest bidder. You have owed forty-five dollars with interest since November 10, 1876. It's now the last of August 1878. You do understand what I've said, don't you Uncle Abe?"

Abraham sensed that something would go wrong. He knew that his purchase of a three-hundred acre tract of land would cause trouble for a colored man. He knew the county officials would keep a close watch on his land. Many of his friends had warned him about his political participation in registering African Americans in the county to vote.

"I talked to Mr. Moore last week about the taxes on this land. He said I could pay it at any time. He gave me his word that I could do this." Abraham implied, a stern look on his face. He knew now that he could trust no one when it came to his land.

"I'm sorry about this Uncle Abram." I was told to come out this morning and give you the letter. Your land was advertised in the Hinesville Gazette. Uncle, I'll tell Mr. Moore you'll be in next Friday to pay your taxes." The short man climbed into his buggy and drove off amidst a strong wind.

Thirty minutes later, Abraham, George, Lewis, and Israel left to work the land they were clearing. They had already cleared fifteen acres of land for cultivation. He needed more time to sell his timber from the land. The trees had to be felled and hauled to a designated location, then hauled to the river to be rafted to the timber market. This was an arduous and time consuming process. Abraham and the workers toiled and labored hard for three hours without a break. They cut down the tall large pine trees and watched them fall to the ground with tremendous force. The sound of axes penetrating the bulky pines fell silent as they took a thirty-minute break.

"Papa I saw you talking with Mr. Eason this morning. What did he want?"

"I hadn't paid the taxes yet. He rode out to remind me. I am going next Friday to pay the taxes on this land."

"Yes sir papa, we is worked too hard to let the buckra take this land. When I gets my land papa, that's the first thing I'm gwine to do is pay the taxes on it. Those buckra think that 'cause we can't read and write like them they can do anything to us."

George observed his father carefully and wanted to be like him in every respect. He admired his father's courage and character. He approved of the way he carried himself when talking to other people and interacting with different people. His father didn't grin and scratch his head when talking to white people as many colored men did. George enjoyed riding with Abraham in his wagon and buggy since he was a small child. He was six years of age when his father joined the Union arm at Savannah in March of 1865.

He was now eighteen years of age and three years under the age of majority. He was of average height, broad-shouldered and powerfully built. He was eager to follow in his father's footsteps. He worked as hard and as swift as anyone that worked with them. Most of all he wanted his father to be satisfied with the work he did.

Two hours later, they had cut down several trees and trimmed the limbs and were taking another break when Mr. Wade walked over to where they rested.

"Hello Uncle Abram, how are you boys doing this afternoon. It looks like y'all getting a lot of work done."

"Yesuh, Mr. Wade we is taking a break now. We's been working hard all day. I need about five more men to help us work and we'll soon have cleared up a lot of land." Abraham said in a sarcastic manner.

"I wanted to talk to George. George, you are a big boy now. Willie tells me you are a hard worker. I heard you are thinking about getting married soon. How would you like to come and work for me?" I'll pay you top wages; ten dollars per month. And you can have an acre of land to plant cotton."

"That sounds good Mr. Wade, but I likes working for my papa." George said, as he looked at Abraham. We is got to finish cutting down dese trees and clearing the land." Mr. Wade was shocked at George's words. He was surprised that George wanted to continue working for Abraham.

The conniving grin was gone from Mr. Wade's face. He appeared stunned by George's words. He wiped his face with his handkerchief as he spoke: "Well George, why don't you think about what I've said. Then let me know how you feel." He looked disappointed at what George told him.

"One other thing before I go, I'll tell you boys this was Indian land hundreds of years ago. The Creek Indians lived here. I told Uncle Abram about it. As you cut down trees and dig up the land you may find artifacts. That is arrow heads and other things that belonged to the Indians. They were called Creek Indians because they lived near the creeks and rivers in this area. I just wanted to tell you that. I'll be seeing you."

Abraham thought to himself, why does he keep reminding us of the Creek Indians and where they lived? George and Israel already know this because I've told them several times and I've told Rilla. Maybe he enjoys telling us about the Indians and where they lived. Well, at least I have a good history lesson about the Creek Indians.

Four weeks later they had cleared another three acres of land. Abraham was excited about the progress they'd made clearing the land. George met and was courting a pretty young lady whom he called Nellie. He had many pleasant things to say about her. He admired her large beautiful brown eyes and her captivating smile. He grew happier with the coming of each new day. He described her to his father who was interested in hearing more about her.

"Papa, she is the girl for me." George said smiling. "I am going to marry her." He said in a joking manner to his father.

"How long have you known her?" Abraham asked.

"Papa, I have seen her 'bout four times. I done met her mama and papa. She is real pretty papa."

"You've seen her just four times and you want to marry her. Does your mama know this? What about Harriet and Macy, have they seen her?"

"No sir papa. She is sixteen; I is three years older than she is."

George was so animated he almost forgot what he had to do. He had been working with Abraham and his younger brother in clearing land on his father's new farm. Frank, Henry, and Luke were working with Henry in helping to construct the log house. They all worked in different areas of the farm. The work was hard and tedious at times, but the men prevailed in getting the job done, piece by piece, and day by day.

George thought of the time he first met Nellie's father and the questions he asked him. Time flew by quickly and he enjoyed talking with her father.

"How old is you young man?" He asked George, with a kind but austere look on his face.

"I'm nineteen Sir, almost twenty."

"Who is some of yo' people? Loance asked as if he knew George's relatives. George felt at ease and not as nervous as he thought he would be.

"My papa's name is Abraham Jackson and my mother's name is Cinderella Jackson; they call her Rilla for short. Some people call papa Abram, or Abe." George spoke proudly of his parents as he spoke.

"I believes I know yo' Papa. That is if he is the person I'se thinking 'bout. I first met him at the courthouse back in sixty-seven. That's when us first got the right to vote. Now that Abe Lincoln's soldiers' is gone us may not be voting long. Those buckra have been trying to stop us from voting." Yo' papa was in Abe Lincoln's army, wasn't he?"

"Yes sir, Mr. Loance. I was six years old when he went to join up." Nellie's father asks a lot of questions George thought to himself. Seconds later, George snapped out of his daydreaming posture and rejoined the others at work.

Whenever he visited Nellie at home Loance sat between them and did most of the talking. Nellie had to remind her father as they talked that George was there to see her. Her mother's name was Charlotte who was invisible most of the time George visited. Loance interrupted George and Nellie frequently talking about farming and the weather. Nellie disliked her papa sitting between them, but was respectful and polite when he spoke. She was highly embarrassed one time when Loance called George, Joseph. Both she and George looked at each other in a stare of silence. George found Nellie to be not as talkative as her father.

Later that evening George told Abraham and Rilla what had happened during the day. He wanted to tell them about his plans to marry Nellie, but was hesitant. Macy and Israel were seeing each other and Harriet met Charles, Nellie's brother and they began seeing each other. They were all talking and making plans but Abraham and Rilla were interested in moving on to their new land. Abraham had cleared thirty-five acres and was ready for cultivation and planting. He also pondered what he would do the upcoming winter. They had felled many large pines that could be floated down the river after the heavy rains of winter set in. He had to prepare for that now, so when the time came he would be ready.

"Rilla, we should be finished with the new house soon. There will be enough room for everyone. How many children do we have now?"

"You know Abram. We is got, let me see now; William is three months old. We have eleven chilun'and three will soon be leaving us. At least, that's what they is saying. Abram, what is you doing with that pencil and paper?" Rilla asked as she saw him with a pencil and a piece of paper in his hand. "You ain't taking lesons from that teacher, Mr. Robinson, Is you?"

"No Cinderella. I'm going to write a letter to an old friend of mine in Charleston. At least he said he was going back to Charleston. We were in the army together. I met him when we were at Battery Wagner. We were mustered out of the Thirty-Third together, twelve years ago."

"How do you know he is still there? Twelve years is a long time."

"I know Rilla, time flies. His papa and momma were sold to a slave Massa in Barnwell in 1859. I didn't have time to talk much, since we were happy to leave Wagner. He may have heard something about my brothers Austin and Henry."

"Abram, you called me Cinderella. You haven't called me Cinderella since before we got married."

"Papa, I didn't know you could write." Harriet interrupted.

"I learned to write my name and the alphabet before I left Savannah. I learned to read a few passages from the good book too. A lot of things your old pappy can do child, you don't know about."

"Papa I ain't heard that word pappy since I was a little girl."

"Harriet, I thought you were watching the little ones. Where is Macy and and Amanda? Y'all make sho' you is watching them chilun.' "I've got to sew this red shirt for yo' papa; Macy you and Tina suppose to be sewing a shirt too, for yo' papa. Why is it taking you so long to do this? You chilun' is so slow. I'se could've sewed two shirts by now. You girls hurry; your papa is a busy man, he's got business to attend to." Rilla smiled as she held up his red shirt.

"You girls hunt me them flour sacks. I is going to make all of you some summer dresses. I seed four of them the other day. I is got to hurry and mend your pappy's shirt."

"Mama, you said that word pappy."

Chapter Seventeen

A petition from eighty seven men of Tattnall County sent to Governor Alfred Colquitt for the issuance of arms and uniforms was rejected by the governor in 1878. Many of the men whose signatures appeared on the petition were former soldiers of the late Civil War. Militia units were being formed and organized by African American men throughout the state of Georgia. Abraham and his friend Jacob were Civil War veterans who were instrumental in organizing the militia unit.

"I heard you boys petitioned the governor for arms and uniforms for your militia unit." John said.

"You heard right John. Aren't you going to join us?" Abraham smiled.

"I was never a soldier. After all, how would it look, a white man in a colored man's militia unit. I'd get run out of the county."

"John, we don't want you to be run out of the county by your own people. We want peace between the whites and the colored people." Abraham said.

"Anyway Uncle, I'm too old to be marching and being fired at. I couldn't walk a half-mile, or even a hundred yards. My feet would ache too badly. You boys have my support."

The presence of African Americans in uniform would result in a culture shock in the small rural county. It was rumored their appearance would engender ill feelings among whites in the county. Abraham believed this was the major reason Governor Colquitt refused to issue them arms. Petitions from throughout the state flooded the governor's office for him to issue arms to African American militia units.

The men soon became discontent waiting to hear positive news coming from the governor. They met and drilled on the eastern fringe of the county. The men had fun waiting for the governor's reply as they marched and drilled in preparation for their trek to the courthouse in Reidsville. A few of the people in the county thought the men were insincere in their efforts to organize a militia unit.

"What's the name of your unit preacher?" Zeke curiously asked.

"Are you talking to me?" Abraham answered.

"We're thinking about calling ourselves the Tattnall Blues."

"Where did you get the name Tattnall Blues from?" Zeke uttered.

"A good many of us wore the blue uniform of the union army. And it was suggested that we call ourselves Tattnall Blues."

Later that day Zell and Jacob arrived at the courthouse while Abraham was checking on his land titles. He and a few of the leading African American men had stirred the curiosity of a few interested whites in the county. Abraham always took George with him when he checked on matters concerning his land. Though George was only nineteen these trips provided him with experience that he'd later need.

"How is your shoulder colonel Jackson," Zell asked in a humorous manner.

"Will it keep you from making the trip to the court house? It's a fourteen mile walk from where we'll start."

"I know that Zell. Have you heard that thirteen years ago I was with the Thirty-Third when we marched from Savannah to Augusta in six days?"

"It may be dangerous papa. All of Abe Lincoln's soldiers have left the county." George interrupted.

"Captain NelsonWhite drilled in us, never back down from a cause when you believe you're right."

Later that afternoon George and Abraham returned home. Before arriving home the two went by to check on the progress that was being made in clearing the land. It rained the early part of the morning; just steady enough to keep Israel, Lewis, and Frank from finishing the task assigned to them by Abraham. He was satisfied with the progress the men had made.

After supper George told Rilla of his plans to get married soon and start on his own.

"Mama, you know that girl that lives about lives about seven miles from here." George smiled. I am going to marry her soon."

"No George, do I know a young lady that lives seven miles from here? How does she look? Is she pretty? Son, you already described her to me didn't you?"

"Yes mama, but I wanted to tell you again."

"Have you told yo' papa about her?"

"Papa knows her papa. They met at the courthouse in sixty-seven, when the coloreds first voted in the county. That's been over ten years ago mama. You know something else: Harriet got eyes for Nellie's brother. They is thinking 'bout getting married."

"Child, your papa doesn't have but one thing on his mind. And that's getting that group of soldiers organized. And he is got this farm on his mind. Clearing land and planting." Rilla grinned.

"That's two things Rilla. Abraham interrupted, rubbing his hands together. After I left Fort Wagner I said I was through with the military."

"But, papa you got to keep on going until you finish." George reminded his father.

"You are right boy. I talked with five of the men that signed the petition. I saw them at the courthouse a few days ago. They were excited and are ready to march."

A week later on a bright sunny morning a group of twenty-five men left their destination and began the fourteen mile march to the courthouse in Reidsville. They sang and marched in complete unison. This was an unprecedented occasion in the history of the small rural county. It was the first time in the county's seventy-seven year history that African Americans had made a protest march to the county seat.

A few people observed the former soldiers and cheered with approval as they marched en route to the courthouse. They were amazed as they observed the African American men as they walked in procession. They were there to give the former soldiers their support. About halfway from the courthouse the men faced opposition and disapproval of their historic march from a small frantic group of former Confederates who disagreed with their cause. They jeered and shouted obscenities at the courageous marchers.

An hour later, the men reached the small wooden courthouse. Again, they were met by a handful of men in Confederate uniforms. Their presence didn't deter the men who were determined to meet with Governor Colquitt. A few of the men were dissipated from a lack of energy. Twelve years had passed since the former union soldiers were mustered out of the army. The group kept its composure as they absorbed racial insults and demeaning words.

Abraham had a letter from a former member of the Thirty-Third regiment United States Colored troops. The former unnamed soldier helped to organize a militia unit in Savannah. In his letter to Abraham his group had written the governor to issue them arms. Abraham and Jacob were prepared to show this letter to the governor.

The men were met on the outside steps by a representative of the governor. Governor Colquitt wasn't present to meet with the men. They gave him a copy of the petition signed by the men who had their signatures affixed to the document. Many of the men were disappointed when they didn't see the governor. He was to give his assent for the men to receive arms and uniforms.

A few white men in the county gave their support for the organization of an African American militia unit. They too were disappointed to learn of the governor's refusal to issue the men arms and uniforms. Abraham, Jacob, Israel, Isaac, and the men who signed the petition were all disappointed. A few White men in the county supported the idea of an African militia unit.

Chapter Eighteen

The coming of spring revealed signs of new life and vitality. Flowers and plants were in full bloom; the birds tweeted and sang; cold nights and cool days gave way to the warmth of spring. Cotton tail rabbits were seen scurrying across the landscape. The Ohoopee was filled with water, near the flood stage. Fruit trees displayed their beautiful picturesque red, white, and pink blossoms.

"Yes sir, papa. Spring is in the air, and I'm so happy." George roared; a grandiose smile on his face. "I am ready to plant my crops." Because of the torrential rain that fell the last few days in February the river overflowed its banks.

George had just turned twenty and was six-feet two inches tall; a strapping, young man. He'd been married for five months to Nellie Eason whom he'd met six months earlier. Nellie had beautiful brown skin and large beautiful brown eyes and had just turned seventeen on January 28th.

Macy and Israel were married in November of 1878; Harriet and Charles Eason were married nearly a year after George and Nellie. Charles was Nellie's older brother. Harriet and Charles met two weeks before George met Nellie.

Later in the afternoon Abraham talked with Lewis and George about a place to build a school. He had already talked to Luke and Israel as to where he wanted to build the school. He had planned for a long time to build a school for the children in the community. Now that he had enough land he was ready to begin planning the location for the school.

Later that evening, toward the end of the work day, Abraham mentioned to Rilla of his plan to erect a school on his newly acquired land. "Rilla, I've been so busy helping to organize the militia, I almost lost count of our chilun.' How many chilun' do we have?" Abraham said jokingly.

"Abram, I knows you ain't forgot. Didn't' you know that Bill was born last May?" And the other chilun' was born befo' you bought de land."

"I know I was here when Bill was born. George, Macy Ann, Harriet and Tina are all married."

"I know I was here when de mid-wife 'livered him. It's the one's dat not married I worries 'bout. You is been talkin' 'bout building a school. We is got enough chilun' to start our own school. When de grand chilun' comes dey'll be going to school too."

"Mama, you and papa have Lewis, Amanda, Nancy, Junior, Amos, Ben, Andrew, and the baby Bill." George interrupted placing his hand on his mother's shoulder.

"Not me, I ain't going to any school." Lewis whispered.

"Bud, when did you come? Where is that pretty wife of yours?"

"Mama, I've been here. And my pretty wife went to see Mrs. Charlotte and Mr. Loance. I am always here mama to help out." George smiled.

"I have been thinking. The governor didn't meet with us because we're colored. Are we a failure?" Abraham asked.

"Some things ain't meant to happen Abram; and I thinks this is one of them."

Chapter Nineteen

Three months later in June of 1879, George and Nellie's first child was born. It was a boy whom they named Elza. Everyone was happy to welcome the new edition to the George and Nellie Jackson family. As Abraham had promised he gave George fifteen acres of land to start his own small farm. He frequently reminded him he had to work hard to become successful just as he did shortly after slavery.

George often sought his father-in-law's advice on the best time to plant his crops. Loance instructed him to plant according to the signs of the zodiac. George learned from Abraham that the best time to plant corn was on dark nights. He was told not to plant anything during the full moon or growing moon.

"I never heard of a growing moon until I was fifteen." George quipped, a puzzled look on his face.

"If you plant during the growing moon you'll get a tall stalk with no ears on it. Now you wouldn't want that to happen. You've got a wife and child to take care of."

Loance had a two hundred-seventy-five acre farm. He had twenty-five cows and two horses and two mules; a surrey buggy and good timber and farm land. He had a large family but was unable to read or write. He yearned for the day he would be able to learn to read and write; especially the Bible. He fully supported the building of the school in which Abraham had planned to construct.

"Well son, I best better be on my way," Loance said as he climbed into his wagon. He had a large red blaze-faced horse and a whip which he popped into the air as he drove off. "I'll see you in a few days. I've got some planting to do myself."

"Okay Mr. Loance," George yelled. "I'll see you soon."

Four weeks later, Abraham, George, Luke, Israel, and sixteen year old Lewis began work to finish the one room log school. Two weeks of intermittent rainfall slowed their progress. Abraham wanted badly to hurry and finish the school. He had seven children under the age of ten and one grandchild fifteen months of age.

The small community was comprised mostly of former slaves and their children. They were isolated from the more distant towns by inadequate transportation and secluded roads. The people and the geography were insulated by winding dusty roads and large tall pines and black gum trees. But the people in the community had one common goal: A burning desire to learn to read and write. The elderly African American men and women often reminded Abraham of a fervent urgency to learn to read the Bible.

Under Abraham's supervision the men hurried to finish cutting the logs to complete the mission. The trees were cut and the logs hauled to the top of the white sand hill where the school was to be built. The work required strong bodies and men with a sense of purpose and dedication to a cause. And that cause which ignited a passion in their hearts was the fear of ignorance. In ten days the one room log school was consummated. The next task was to construct small benches for the little children and larger benches and desks for the larger kids. A large wood-burning heater was placed in the center of the large one-room building.

The new school was ready to open on the last day of October 1879. It was a crude building with picturesque scenery. As Abraham later recalled, it was Indian summer and the pretty colorful wildflowers had disappeared. Tall pines surrounded the building on both sides of the school; colorful redbirds, blue jays, red breast robins, and other smaller birds presented a scenic view for the students, teachers, and visitors. Israel pointed out to Abraham and Loance after the first day of school one had to be present to enjoy the colorful birds even in October.

The school was located ten miles northwest of the county seat. It was named for its organizer and architect, Abraham Jackson. The first day of school saw children come from as far as ten miles away. Many of them walked and a few rode in wagons with a parent, grandparent, or relative. The hunger and thirst to learn to read and write had reached its zenith. The announcement of the opening of a new school for colored children had been discussed in the county for several weeks. Children of all shapes, proportions, heights, and manner of dress descended on the large one room school on a cool morning.

The dream of learning to read and write for former slaves: Both parents and grandparents and other relatives was now a reality. Parents and grandparents wanted their offspring to achieve what they'd been denied by law for centuries. A state of illiteracy had handicapped the African American. The twin evils of slavery and illiteracy had prevented them from being equals with their fellow white citizens. The African American was cheated out of his land and wages because of his illiteracy. They were unable to vote, serve on juries, and give testimony against whites in court. The Civil Rights Act of 1866 and the passage of the Fourteenth and Fifteenth Amendments did little to change the status of the African American in Georgia.

With a spirited longing to learn to read and write; a few of the older people came to school with the younger ones. They had one thing in mind, and that was to learn to read the Bible. God had granted them their freedom and they wanted to give reverence to him by learning to read his word.

The first day of school was a get acquainted day and a time for the teacher to learn the names of all the students who came that day. Most of the students who came that day were energetic and bright-eyed and had pleasing smiles. They were the children of the Jacksons, Easons, Smiths, Collins, Sikes, and Lanier families. A good many of the children came to school dressed in raggedy clothes and shoes. This was a sign of the abject poverty in the area that followed the Civil War and Reconstruction in Georgia.

A week later the children and three older students were there to explore and acquire new information about their environment. Their teacher was energetic and enthusiastic about the work the children had to learn and retain. The children were to learn how to write their names; the alphabet, simple reading and writing, and simple arithmetic. The grades were from one through six. As they advanced and mastered the material; the students advanced to a higher level. In fifth and sixth grades they were taught geography, arithmetic, spelling, and United States history.

The student's first teacher was Israel Fraser. He was married to Abraham's second oldest daughter Macy Ann. Israel was a thin man of medium height and had long black sideburns and a thin black beard. He was a distinguished looking man with a lucid voice and had a cheerful demeanor. He worked helping Abraham, George, Lewis and Luke in the construction of the school. It was said that Israel acted as the building planner of the one-room school. He was a self-taught and self-educated man. He had a large brown mule he called "Pomp."

The majority of the children came to school cheerful and full of energy. It was a difficult time for many of the children whose parents were sharecroppers and not as upbeat as some. Few African Americans in the county had their own land or farms. These parents and grandparents held a different view about the educational success of their children. They believed their children wouldn't succeed because of their poverty and the Jim Crow laws they faced.

They believed since the federal troops left the county African Americans had little chance to advance beyond their present state of benign poverty.

Abraham, Loance, Aberdeen, and Israel talked to the skeptical parents about the importance of first learning to read and write and extending their education. An inconsiderable number of men agreed with Abraham that an education was important and that their children needed the knowledge and skills to progress even in an era in which African American boys and girls were plagued by racism and Jim Crow laws.

"All of de older people I talks to wants to learn to read de Bible and learn how to write dere names. I doesn't know 'bout white chilun' coming here to your school Mr. Jackson"

"First, Albert it's not my school. It's a school for everyone in the community. Anyone is welcome to come to this school. Slavery is over. We are free people and you can't be free if you can't read or write."

"I don't need no eddication, I knows how to plow a mule. I knows how to plant corn and cotton. My boss, Mr. Peters says learning to read and write is a waste of time. My chilun ain't gwine to no school." John Henry muttered.

"If you can't read, how will you know when you're being cheated? If you can't read anyone can tell you anything. Well Albert, you don't want that to happen." Israel said. "Listen to me, please listen. During slavery you could be bought and sold and nothing could be done about it. Am I right? You had no rights. If old Massa caught you with a book, you could be whipped. The worst thing that could happen, you could be sold, separated from your wife or children." But now your only slave Massa is your mind."

A few share croppers expressed opposition to an education and stubbornly detested the idea of becoming literate. Mr. Fraser was a resourceful teacher and used numerous techniques and strategies to get his pupils to learn. At the end of the week leading up to Thanksgiving some of the parents who were opposed to their children attending the new school after studying the options became receptive to the idea. After probing the mental picture of acquiring more knowledge and becoming literate versus being unlearned their choice became simple.

A Thanksgiving Day celebration was held at the school for everyone in the close-knit community. The first of its kind and a large number of people even a few Caucasians attended the unprecedented occasion. This event showed that the process of reconciliation had surpassed for the moment the bitter feelings that divided the two races. Two years had passed since the federal troops left the county. The feeling Abraham once entertained about white people had diminished. But he was still cautious in his business dealings with those who had treated him with disdain during slavery. Having learned the alphabet and how to read and write his name and the simple elements of an education while with the Thirty-Third Regiment, United States Colored Troops, he was eager and upbeat at the opening of the new school.

At daybreak, George, Lewis, Israel, and Frank went hunting for deer, wild turkey, and rabbits. An hour later they'd traveled nearly two miles before they saw their first deer. The swift-footed animal was out of range before a shot could be fired. The speedy deer was too quick for the slow-firing shotgun used by the impatient hunters. Two hours after their arrival in the woods they were able to shoot two wild turkeys and six rabbits. George and the three other men were embarrassed at being unable to kill a deer. They were animated and thankful for the game they'd captured.

The Thanksgiving Day feast was to begin at 1:00 clock p.m. that afternoon. This would grant everyone who came from a distance a time to eat, get together, and return home before dark. This aggregation of men and women was a phenomenal gathering as they exchanged tales, ideas, and stories of interest about their past, present, and future. The occasion gave the women a chance to entertain each other and to talk about husbands and boyfriends. Most of all, it gave them a chance to exchange ideas about their cooking ventures and sewing techniques.

Tables were set twenty yards long, with many different kinds of foods; turkey, chicken, sweet potatoes, rice, corn, and beans. For dessert they had apple, sweet potato, and peach pies. The aroma of the food could be detected as far as a mile away. Everyone gathered around the lengthy tables to await the blessing of the food. They were delighted to begin eating their Thanksgiving dinner. Loance Eason, George's father-in-law and a key person in favor of the establishment of the school gave the Thanksgiving Day blessing of the food. His supplication was reverent but yet simple. He thanked God for all the blessings He'd granted them. He asked his blessing on the food and the continual blessing for the success of the new school. And he asked God to give them the wisdom and the courage to face the hardships of the present and the future.

Chapter Twenty

Two months later on a cold January day in 1880 the water in the narrow road had turned to ice. Abraham didn't leave home until three hours after daybreak. Earlier George and Lewis had checked on the farm animals and provided them with hay and fodder. They left home in the frigid January temperature. The younger children didn't attend school because of the extremely cold weather. The ice had begun to slowly melt as the temperature began to rise above the freezing mark.

About a mile from his home Abraham met a man whom he attended church with. He called the man Handy. "Hello brother Abe, how is you and the boys doing on this cold day?"

"Just common, how are you? What are you doing out here this early in the morning?"

"I show don't know. I was in that little town yesterday; that town dat's 'bout three miles south of here. Brother Abe, You know it's cold enough to kill hogs."

"The boys and I are just checking our fence. It looks like someone pushed down the rails for about twenty yards. These roads are so narrow it's hard to travel on them."

"I heard you had a Thanksgiving feast at your school before Christmas. How is your school coming along? If we don't start a fire, we's gwine to soon freeze. I'd betta get going brother Abe. I'll see you soon."

"I'll see you later. I've got to go to Reidsville soon to check my land titles. I'll see you later."

"Papa, it's too cold to do anything. My hands is about to freeze. Lewis' hands are so cold they look frozen in his pockets."

"Let's go boys before old Bob freezes. If Old Bob freezes we can't get back home. Rilla won't know what happened to us."

"I knows papa. Nellie and Elza won't know where we is."

Six months later, On July 22, 1880, Rilla gave birth to a baby boy. They named him Millard. He was born a healthy baby and was large in size. She was proud of the newborn infant and swore to the midwife Milly, he would be the last.

"Here is a ham Milly, take this and you and Jim enjoy it." Rilla said as Harriet handed the ham to her.

"I want you to make me some of that lye soap when you gets a chance. I'll send Lewis for it on Friday. That'll give you enough time to make it. If you need something else I will send it by Nancy." Rilla echoed.

Milly was the midwife in the community and delivered most of the babies. She smoked a pipe and wore a blue bonnet which she said gave her luck. Most of the children in the community gave her a strange stare when she was around with her funny looking pipe with the smoke shooting up out of it.

"Don't hurry Milly." Rilla said. "You can spend the night if you'd like. Abraham can milk the cow in the morning; Macy Ann will be here and she can cook some biscuits. I can't do nuttin'now, but I'll be able to later on." Rilla was excited; she had an energized look on her face.

George had an old hound dog called "Rabbit." He was slow-footed and George teasingly referred to him as Rabbit. When he went hunting the fleet-footed rabbits would leave his dog far behind in the chase. After he returned from hunting on Saturday mornings he had Nellie to help him clean the furry animals. His hunting trip yielded him four rabbits. Nellie was curious at what she had seen as she arrived to help George clean the rabbits. She observed a beautiful horse hitched to a wagon on the east side of the house. She walked up to the large animal, gazing at its large size.

"That's a pretty mule there. Whose is it I wonder?"

"That's papa's horse. It's not a mule. Horses are larger than mules; at least most of 'em is. That ain't no pretty horse; that's old "Skipper." George laughed.

"What kind of name is that for a hoss? Papa gots a hoss he calls Jeff and a mule he calls David.

"Skipper: I ain't heard no name like that for a hoss."

George was still laughing as he tried to explain how the well-proportioned animal got its name. "Papa gave him that name 'cause when he first hitched him to a wagon, he trotted like he was skipping.

"How can you tell whether he is a boy hoss or a girl hoss?" Nellie asked.

George felt embarrassed as he struggled to answer her question. The laughing stopped. "Well, Nell, it's like this. You see uh—well a boy horse; you can tell by looking uh. There is papa I wonder where he is going. I'll tell you later Nell, we've got to clean these rabbits. Let me show you what to do."

"Why can't you tell her Bud? Now is as good a time as ever."

"But papa we got to skin these rabbits. I'll tell her the next time I go hunting."

"George: I know the difference between a boy hoss and a girl hoss. I jest wanted to see what you'd say. Papa got two mules and two hosses. And Bud you've seen the four of them." Nellie smirked.

"Nellie, where is Elza?"

"You forgot. Easter is looking after him." Nellie muttered.

"Who is Easter?" George seriously asked.

"She is my baby sister. You is asking too many questions. I is going to see your mama and her new baby. Do you want me to tell her that you don't know the difference between a girl hoss and a boy hoss."

"Nellie, the word is horse not hoss. You need to go to the school and let Mr. Fraser teach you. Mr. Loance is going to school. He told me he wants to learn to read the Bible."

A week later, Nellie traveled to visit her mother Charlotte. She took one year old Elza to see her. She had tears running down the side of her cheeks as she approached her mother. Charlotte was washing clothes when Nellie arrived in the wagon.

"What's wrong Nell?" Charlotte asked as the wagon came to a complete stop.

"I don't know mama. My baby is burning up wid a fever."

"Yes, he is hot Charlotte said" in a faint voice.

"Bring 'em inside. Us will git sometin' for him. 'Member Nell, when Easter was sick wid de feber. And when Charles was seven, my mama told me what to give 'em. God bless the dead; his feber was worse than Elza's. Nell, my grand mama told me 'bout an old Indian remedy. She told me to go into the woods and git some rabbit droppings; it ain't nutin' but green weeds and grass. You have to boil it in hot water; and then give a pinch of it to the baby. Don't forget to put a little sugar in it; it will git rid of dat feber."

"But mama, he's too young. Can I do that and will it work?" Nellie asked.

"My old grand mammy, dey say was mixed wid Indian blood; she was close to a hundred years old when she died. I gits sick one time and my old Massa's wife had her to git some rabbit tobacco leaves and boil 'em. I drinks dat tea; child, dat tea was bitter as gall. Dat tea makes me well and I ain't been sick since.

"Mama, you talks so long. I think he's better. Look at 'em, he is smiling."

Two hours later Nellie and Elza returned home. George was in the field plowing and wondered what happened to them. The August sun was extremely hot and humid. Nellie explained everything that had happened to him when he came in from the field. She was happy and a bundle of joy. She told George about Ezla's fever and what her mother had given him to drink for it. The Indian remedy had quickly relieved his inflamed temperature. George knew about the rabbit tobacco mixture because he and Harriet took the solution when they were sick. The boiling of green pine straw needles and rabbit tobacco tea were the solutions to a fever. George hadn't ever heard that the green grass in rabbit dropping eradicated fever in a baby.

Later that night George and Nellie enjoyed the light of the August moon. Elza was asleep and felt much better. Both were happy to see the day come to an end and enjoy each other's presence. They both sat outside enjoying the singing of the whip-poor-will.

"How quiet and peaceful the night is." George said gazing up into the starry sky.

"Yes, the moon show is bright tonight," Nellie said; just like the middle of the day. The stars are shining bright George. Look at 'em; how do you say that word?" "It is twinkle. I learned that word from papa."

"All of the birds, except that old whip-poor-will are quiet tonight. Little Elza and all the other birds is asleep."

"I heard papa talking to a buckra earlier this morning 'bout a cow some colored man stole. Papa tickled me. He asked the buckra man a question. Papa told the man he would talk to this Byrd man about the cow and see if he would return it."

"Is that all Mr. Abraham did is talk to the man?"

"Yes, the people around here believe papa is a man of his word. It's getting late Nell, let's go inside and check on little Elza. Let's see if he is asleep. I've got a busy day ahead of me tomorrow."

"George, I wonder how many stars is there up in that big sky?" Nellie smiled."

"I don't know, but if you count 'em, let me know. I think it would take you 'bout ten years to find all of them. That is if you count 'bout a thousand stars per night."

"Spose, just 'spose it's too dark and you can't see any."

"That means you have to count twice as many. And that would take you twenty years. Mr. Fraser, Israel, mace's husband, the teacher up at the school is teaching me my time tables. It's time to go to bed."

George the eldest son of Abraham and Rilla lived a simple life on the fifteen acres he received from his father. Both he and Nellie were born into slavery; he was born in 1859 and she was born in 1862. Both were born in the month of January. Loance teased them about being the Emancipation Proclamation babies. Both came of age during the aftermath of Reconstruction. They knew the importance of dignity and self-respect in a state and nation in which African Americans were treated as second class citizens. Lynching and violence were a part of the state's shameful history. The two of them yearned to be literate and wished the same for everyone in their small close-knit community.

Much of his fifteen acres had to be cleared for planting crops. He had only cleared seven of his fifteen acres. Cotton was the chief money crop at the time; as it had been before the Civil War and in the aftermath of the war. He worked with Abraham in clearing land, he had to cut trees and remove the stumps before the plowing and cultivation of the new ground for planting.

Harriet and Tina's husbands Charles Eason and Abraham Tillman helped George, along with Frank and Henry, until Frank purchased his farm, afterward's he worked with both Abraham and George. They cut the virgin timber from the woods and hauled it to the loading point where it was floated downstream into the Ohoopee River and into the Altamaha. The rafting of timber was an adventure for most of the younger men engaged in the business. Especially when the weather was pleasant and the rafts didn't rip apart by hitting a rock or sandbar.

During late winter around the second week of March the wind blew strongly across the plowed fields. Dust covered the area and one's visibility was limited. Farm work was a fulltime job during the planting and harvesting season. George was usually up at daybreak, tended to his farm animals and by the time he'd eaten lunch the powerful March wind had diminished. Later they regained strength and the dust again covered the plowed fields.

Again during spring the flowers and trees took on new life and were swarming with beautiful blossoms. The birds sang with joy as the warmth of spring ushered in a feeling of esthetic renewal; everything took on new life. The rabbits, squirrels, and other wildlife in the woods were energized and excited with the coming of spring. Again George's dog "Rabbit" had fun chasing rabbits through the woods and trailing twenty yards behind them. George had fun watching his dog trying to catch the speedy rabbits.

Chapter Twenty-One

Four years later Abraham's children had grown older. His youngest daughter Idella was seven years of age; his two youngest sons William and Millard were five and three years of age respectively. Lewis, his second oldest son turned twenty in December. Amanda was fifteen years of age. They attended the one room log school up on the white sand hill. The school attendance had doubled since its establishment four years earlier in 1879. The children enjoyed attending school and learning to read and write. They also enjoyed arithmetic and geography. Their history class had been suspended and their teacher concentrated on geography as their most important social studies lesson.

The number of adults interested in learning to read the Bible significantly increased. Their passion for learning was matched only by their time and energy. A few learned to read the Bible, write their names, and learned the alphabet and that completed their elementary learning. The idea of attending school with young children was no inconvenience nor did it discourage them. The greatest challenge for the teacher at the school was to transform the thinking of disinterested, skeptical, and irresolute parents.

Abraham's experience during the bitter years of slavery forced him to have an irresistible urge to learn to read and write. His experience with being illiterate changed his way of thinking about the fallacy of learning and the attainment of knowledge. He often asked himself, would his passion for learning to read and write be as strong had he not spent time in the Union army? Was it luck or providence that allowed him to purchase over three hundred acres of land for farming and the construction of the School building? These thoughts pestered him as he reflected on family life and the success of African Americans and Caucasians living together in close proximity as a society.

Two years later in June 1885, Abraham was ordained to the ministry in a local Caucasian church. Prior to this he attended an African American church ten miles from his residence. His request to move his membership to a church closer to his residence benefited him greatly. This move by Abraham was historic. He became the first African American licensed to preach and conduct services in an all white church in the county. He was warmly received by the white congregation.

A scant number of African Americans joined as members to support him. Rilla and her mother Milly became members of the church and two of their relatives. African Americans in the community referred to him as Elder Abraham Jackson and a few Whites in their oral communication with him addressed him as "Uncle Abraham." Thirteen African Americans became members of this diminutive log church located in the Northeastern part of Tattnall County approximately ten miles from the county seat.

Rilla and all of her children were proud and overjoyed to know that he had been ordained to preach the gospel at this church. His family was happy for him to undertake the duties and responsibility as a minister of the gospel. Rilla frequently reminded him to look his best when going to preach the gospel.

"You is a preacher now, at that white church; You is got to look your best and do your best. What you need is a pretty black suit." Rilla admonished him.

"Yes mama, papa needs a black suit or a dark suit." Harriet interrupted.

"Child, them suits cost a lot of money," Tina advised.

"Papa can get a good suit for 'bout five dollars" Lewis said.

"Where can you get a suit for five dollars? It won't be anywhere in Tattnall County. Trust me. Papa would have to go to Savannah or Augusta. He may be able to find one in Hinesville."

"Ah. Listen at that school teacher talk." George smiled. "He knows his geography. I told Mace and Harriet they need to let Mr. Israel teach them." George chuckled.

"Listen children. I have a black suit and a navy blue suit and I think they look great. I have had these suits a long time. I've had them since I joined Eden Church in 1880. I will be fine."

"You preach to them buckra folks and you want to look your best." Rilla said looking at Abraham's suits. You've got a hole in your left coat pocket. And the right pocket is torn."

"Rilla, the clothes don't make the preacher. The good Lord calls the preacher. And he will provide for him." Abraham instructed everyone. "The white folk is just like the colored folk; they all want to hear a word from the Lord. God made us all in His image and in his likeness." Abraham saluted, placing his hand on his Bible.

Rilla and Nellie had been talking to Charlotte about making Abraham a beautiful white shirt. Loance mentioned to Abraham that Nellie and Charlotte said they had a surprise for him. But he had no idea what the surprise was. The idea was mostly Nellie's. She'd wanted to do something for "Mr. Abraham," as she called him.

The next day the conversation continued about Abraham's attire. He, Benjamin, Andrew, (whom everyone referred to as General), and Abraham Jr. had just returned home from the field. The boys unhitched the two horse wagon and placed the animals in the barn.

"How about a beautiful black suit mama." Nancy said looking at her father. "That would look good on you papa; Lewis' girlfriend's mama know a tailor Mr. Smith. I heard he is a good Tailor."

"You needs a good pair of shoes too papa." Lewis argued.

"You have got to get Miss Charlotte to make you that blue dress Rilla."

"How did you know 'bout that Abe uh—I means Elder Jackson."

"I told everyone yesterday that I don't need all of those things. Now, let's change the conversation and talk about something else."

"You is got to get Miss Charlotte to make you that new dress Mama."

"Papa, where did those free colored people go to church? The one's everyone called free niggers. You said change the conversation."

"Papa, he means the uppity high class, high yellar colored people. The one's who is in the same class as the poor Injuns in this county." Tina said.

"Tina, where did you come from? Don't look like I know who will come from where. Where did you come from? Yes, those people were never slaves. I heard they owned land and farms as far back as the 1840s and 1850s. And their children, we don't call them high yellows or whatever you . . . are saying." Elder Jackson cautioned them.

"Where is Lewis?" Rilla asked. "He and General suppose to go with me to Milly's tomorrow."

"Mama, Lewis and General suppose to go with Papa to get a wagon wheel tomorrow."

"You know Lewis is twenty-three now. He is now courting or calling on Mrs. And Mr. Brewton's daughter." Harriet snarled."

"Which of their daughters' is you talking about? They ain't got but one daughter; the one they call Ann Jane. I seed her the other day and she is pretty."

"Is she as pretty as George's wife? Soon Nancy, Amanda, Benjamin, and little Abram will be looking for husbands and wives."

Early the next morning before daybreak Abraham, Lewis, and General, traveled to pick up a wagon wheel and a plow. At the supply store Abraham saw his friend Jake. He was there to pick up a new plow as well as a wagon wheel.

"Hello Abraham. I mean Elder Jackson. I ain't seen you since the march to the courthouse. What is you doing now? Is you farming for Mr. Collins or do you have your own place?"

"No, Jake I got my own place now. Me and my boys been grubbing and clearing land."

"Abram, how many boys do you have now? The last talk I had wid you, you told me you had five young men. How many do you have now?"

"I have seven sons and seven daughters."

"Seven sons and seven daughters, Elder Abraham, you remind me of Abraham of the Bible. A nation will come out of your lions; seven sons and seven daughters. You are blessed."

Two hours later Abraham and his sons returned to his farm. It was a cloudy mild day. The small rural community was growing and the people in Abraham's neighborhood, both African American and Caucasian were growing closer together. The sparsely populated area was a close-knit locale.

Midway between Reidsville and Abraham's residence the threat of rain was in the air. The faint sound of thunder was heard about a mile away. This warning of rain was short, immediate, and unforeseeable. The morning was quiet and peaceful. A small wind blew in a southeasterly direction, but there was no visible threat of rain other than a remote clap of thunder. Abraham was home within an hour of leaving Reidsville. Skipper didn't pull the wagon today, his work task was reserved mostly for church and important business dates.

When Abraham returned home he saw Rilla and Milly talking to six-year old Millard. Milley lived with Frank and his wife and children. She visited Rillia and Abraham when she was needed by her mother. Milly was sixty-six years of age and was as agile and full of energy as when she was in her thirties. She appeared nervous and disturbed about something.

"Abram, I don't know what's wrong wid your child. I told Rilla he might be having some kind of spell. So I ain't getting too close to him. Rilla sent for me this morning. The boy may be afflicted wid some kind of evil spirit. You is a preacher now and you can pray for him." Milly suggested.

"An evil spirit, no such thing; the child is burning up with a fever. Feel his face and little hands Rilla." Abraham was nervous and thought that Rilla and her mother would know what to give the child.

"I tell you what you can do Rilla," get a wet cloth and rub it against his head. Isn't there some rabbit tobacco growing somewhere in the woods; get some, boil the leaves and let him drink. And that should cure his fever."

"Miss Milly: You don't really believe that my boy has an evil spirit, do you? That can't happen. He just has a fever from maybe eating something he shouldn't have."

Abraham remembered when he first received his call to preach the experience he had. He recalled the nightmares of slave life and how it affected his mind. But evil spirits he couldn't imagine. He awakened one night just after three hours of sleep. Sweat trickled down his body. He'd told only Rilla of his vision of a large ball of fire moving across the Western sky. This ball of fire landed in the top of his trees and burned them all up. And another incident happened to him which was no dream, vision, or nightmare. When he was coming from visiting George's father-in-law, Loance, he'd just fed his horse, Old Skipper. Suddenly, a chain wrapped tightly around both his ankles and he couldn't move. He remembers being paralyzed with fear until he heard Lewis call his name and ask him what was wrong. After that night he became less pretentious and he knew what he'd been called to do.

Abraham awakened early the next morning. He didn't want to reveal his dream to Rilla or as he called it—his vision. He knew now without hesitation, God had revealed Himself to him. This was no supernatural imagination or apparition he faced but the spiritual revelation of God. He now had more confidence to counsel people who came to him with problems. He cautioned both black men and white men to be more open in their relationships with each other. He admonished them to be more courageous and to stand up for righteousness.

Abraham had heard those with less courage and little foresight tell him almost daily that the Ku Klux Klan and other night riders would terrorize him and other colored people in the community. He often stressed to the African American men to have courage and stand up and resist the evil forces in their county and community. He stressed to men of wisdom and courage in the community and county not lose hope and faith in their challenge to do right. He summoned each man not to be capricious, but unwavering in their bid to overcome injustice and evil.

This was Elder Jackson's third year in the ministry at Cedar Creek. The members continued to warmly receive him and give him their support. He was frequently away from home on the weekends. He and his large red-blazed faced horse Skipper left home on Friday and wouldn't return until late Sunday afternoon. He would place a bale of hay and two bundles of fodder in the rear of his buggy and bid farewell to Rilla and his younger children. His travels sometimes took him into distant parts of the county, to many small unincorporated towns all located in Tattnall County, the fourth largest county in the state in 1887.

When he returned on Sunday afternoons, Rilla and the children were eager to greet him. He and Skipper were a sight to behold. Elder Jackson had all kinds of food and meats in his black red-wheeled buggy. There were collard greens, mustard, molasses, cabbage, sweet potatoes and different kinds of meat. He wouldn't accept money from his church family members. This practice continued for Elder Abraham Jackson throughout his church ministry. He would often kid everyone: "God has already paid me; I am alive and in good health."

Chapter Twenty-Two

George's first born child, Elza, was eleven and his daughter Ida was two. Ida was born in April of 1888. Abraham's two youngest sons William and Millard were twelve and ten years of age respectively. Time moved rapidly and the close-knit community of Jacksontown was quickly growing with it. The influx of turpentine workers and farmers were moving into the area as well. The county was located in the Pine Barrens region of Southeast Georgia and was approximately sixty-five miles west of Georgia's oldest and second largest city. The region depended upon the virgin timber, especially the tall pines, and agriculture for its sustenance. Several African American moved into the county to work turpentine; that is to remove or extract what was called tar from the pine trees. Many migrated into the county to work in cotton. They came into the county from North and South Carolina.

Harriet and Charles had a ten year old son James, born in 1880. When Abraham and George had business to attend at the county seat Benjamin was placed in charge of the work that needed to be done. He was seventeen and a well-disciplined and responsible young man. Abraham Jr. had married and moved away to Savannah. Amanda and Nancy were twenty-two and twenty years of age, but still lived at home. Andrew nicknamed "General" was sixteen years of age.

Abraham and George when they went to the courthouse usually traveled together in George's buggy. It seemed as if they were forever checking their land acreage to make sure it was accurately and properly recorded. They left for the courthouse and arrived an hour later. George drove his buggy and his big brown horse called "Brownie." His horse "Brownie" reminded him of his father's massive horse "Skipper." George had been uneasy for days about his newly purchased land. After finishing their business they were ready to return to the small community newly called Jackson Town. The ten mile return trip was done in less than two hours. They stopped along the way to give "Brownie" a rest from pulling the heavy load.

The one room log school was ten years old and would be eleven in October 1890. The children attended school there from all of the surrounding towns and areas. The farthest distance a child had to walk was a ten mile radius in each direction from the point of the school. The students now had books and paper to aid them in their learning. The number of adult students attending to learn to read and write had fallen to three.

The next week Abraham and his boys prepared to cut timber and load it on the timber carts and haul it to the point where it could be taken to the river and made into rafts. Heavy rain had fallen in December and continued into the New Year. It hadn't rained in seven days and the first thing Monday morning they were ready to begin work. The wind blew strongly all day Sunday diminishing Sunday night. The previous week the ground was saturated with water and the roads were boggy. George and Lewis traveled the route in the wagon the path they would cross to get the logs to the drop off point near the river. They checked to see if the route was passable for them and the animals.

"Papa we checked the route we are to take to the river. It's too boggy for now. We should wait at least two more days. I think we should wait at least until Wednesday." George said.

"George is right papa. We need to wait at least until Wednesday." Lewis agreed.

"Well, Bud, if it rains again and the road freezes, what do we do?" Abraham pointed out. Frank and Henry said they would help this week. I don't know if Andy will be available."

"Papa, what about General and Ben: They can help us." Lewis pointed out.

George nodded in agreement. "What about that old Cherokee Indian man. Why don't you ask him? He helped us before, but I couldn't understand a word he said."

"We'll have enough. Can Ben and General swim? That water gets rough the further you get towards that bigger river. I remember what happened to Henry before we were freed. When those logs hit a sandbar, they tore loose and pinned him against a root, he almost drowned." Abraham cautioned them.

"Papa, we forgot to tell you. The main road, the one that we travel to get to the loading point is washed out." Lewis informed Abraham.

"How could you boys forget that? Now, we are going to have to build a new road. It shouldn't take too long. An old Indian trail leads to the river. It's about a half-mile longer. George how long do you think that'll take."

"If all of us work we should finish in less than seven days." That is if it don't rain or snow." George grinned. "That'll be something papa that Ben and General can help us do."

Rafting timber down the Ohoopee River was an adventurous as well as a daring trip. The weak and frail stayed away or shunned such an arduous task. Abraham knew all of his boys and those who worked before with him "running the rivers" as it was called wasn't an easy task. He knew about the wild tales that were told about both rivers. The tale of seeing bears ten feet tall and big cats that swam in the water looking for victims to attack. He assured his boys and those that worked with him that these were all tall tales. He'd seen a catamount one time walking along the banks of the Ohoopee River. But he hadn't seen any bears. Although there had been tales of the sighting of bears, Abraham explained to his younger children that he hadn't seen any.

The next day was cold and windy. The wind blew in gusts until mid morning and then diminished later as it returned to normal. Abraham was anxious to get started building the alternative road that led to the river. The ground was still soggy but had begun to dry out. The men had cleared a good stretch of the road that led to their destination by mid afternoon.

"Papa, if we continue to work, it may not take us seven days." George said, wiping the sweat from his forehead. What happened to Lewis and Uncle Frank?"

"They had to go and get some more shovels and picks. And they had to get more water too; the wind blew our water over."

"Papa, I saw you holding your shoulder. What's wrong?" Ben asked.

"It'll be alright. I guess old age is creeping up on me. I've had trouble with that shoulder since I left Battery Wagner in 1866. I hope Lewis and Frank get back soon. We got a lot of work to do."

The temperature had risen a little and the wind was calm as the men took a break from their laborious work. Abraham and George wanted to be assured that their alternative route was wide enough for the oxen and mules to pull the logs to the landing to be placed into the river. This type of work required strong animals to pull the timber to its designated location and the men had to guide the undisciplined beasts.

A week later the road was cleared enough for passage to the river and the land was dry. Abraham and his three sons along with Frank, Henry, Cherokee, and Andy began the trek to the river. They began their day's work a little after daybreak. Halfway downstream two of the rafts ran into heavy rocks and split apart and they had to work hard swimming in the cold water to recover the logs. It took them all afternoon to retrieve the logs and tie them together again before they could move on. It was an eight hour journey down the Ohoopee and the Altamaha. They had to spend the night in the small town and return home the next day. Their return trip from Darien took the entire day to get back to Tattnall County. Abraham swore this was his last trip rafting timber downstream. His bones were getting too old to travel such a distance rafting timber.

Elder Jackson enjoyed his trek to McIntosh County. It was a complete contrast to Tattnall County. Tattnall had no African Americans in their local government. The county had only one state senator. Who represented their interest during the Reconstruction Era and he was Tunis G. Campbell. He represented Liberty, McIntosh, and Tattnall. In their local government McIntosh had an African American sheriff, Clerk of the Courts, a County Ordinary, and men that represented the county in other local areas. The county had three African American state representatives. Abraham enjoyed talking about the contrast of people and ideas.

Although he was a member of the Cedar Creek primitive Baptist Church he still continued to travel to Eden one Sunday out of the month and to Cedar Creek. He also attended other local churches in and out of the county.

Abraham decided to build a church on his land in Jackson Town in 1891. After a meeting with the church leaders of other primitive Baptist faiths, Elder Jackson decided to build a church on his land. The church was built near the school. He supervised the building of the church and furnished the logs for the construction of the church. Elder Jackson, Rilla, Milly, George, Nellie, Macy, and Israel were in the organization of the church.

They agreed to have service on the second Sunday of each month. Elder Jackson continued to attend service at Eden and Cedar Creek. As he was riding in his buggy one Sunday morning on his way to Eden, he decided to stop and give his horse a rest.

He got down from his buggy and hitched Tom, his new horse, to a hitching post; he walked across the road to get a bucket of water for his horse. On his way back to the buggy he was met by three white men. One of the men bumped into him in an attempt to intimidate the quiet spoken preacher.

"Nigger, why don't you watch where you are going." The man looked at Elder Jackson for a moment, and then spat a big wad of tobacco juice from his mouth. "You ain't from 'round here, is you boy?" The two other men cheered him own as he hurled insults and racial slurs at Elder Jackson.

"My name is Elder Abraham Jackson and I am not a nigger or a boy. I am a minister of the gospel. And I am on my way to church at Eden." Elder Jackson did not bat an eye. He gave Tom a pail of water. He wore his navy blue suit and had on a dark blue shirt and black tie.

"We was jest having a little fun, preacher. You ain't like the niggers we know. That's a pretty horse and buggy you got there. Go ahead on preacher to your church."

Divine providence must have intervened on Elder Jackson's behalf. He left the little place and went on to church and had an incredible time. He didn't have any more trouble from anyone in the area. He stopped and rested his horse and then returned home before night. Elder Jackson began to notice a difference in the racial climate between the African Americans and Caucasians in his community and surrounding areas in the county.

He arrived home two hours after he left church. Except for the incident he experienced on his way to church, he enjoyed a pleasant time the remainder of the day. Upon his arrival home, Abraham had Bill and Millard to take care of "Tom". He wanted "Tom" to have a full measure of water, grain, and hay.

Rilla asked him how was church and his trip to Eden. He made known to her that he was happy and in good spirits about his trip and what transpired at church. He told her of the unpleasant encounter he had just before he arrived at church. Harriet and Charles had come to visit just before he arrived back home. George and Nellie came shortly after his return home.

"Papa, Mr. Loance had a stroke yesditty." Harriet lamented.

"How is he doing?" Abraham asked. "Was he at home or where was he?"

"We didn't ask Easter. She told us about it. He must have had a light stroke; if not someone would've let us know something." Charles peered.

"How old is Mr. Eason Nellie?" Abraham asked.

"I don't rightly know, but he is up in age. I heard him say he was forty-two when I was born. My mama says I is thirty-two now. So he must be right at seventy or something."

"Well, we is all growing older; I mean we ain't as young as we use to be."

"Mr. Loance is tough he'll be okay." George muttered. "He still can outrun me and lift a log that's too heavy for me. I saw him chasing after his old bull the other day."

"Papa, I heard you are going to build a church up close to the school. I heard you is already picked out the trees you are going to use to build it with"

"I'm glad you heard all of those things George. But I haven't heard that much. Yeah, we need to get started soon. I am getting too old to be going back and two to some of the places I'm going."

Four months later the new church in Jackson Town was constructed. Everyone in the neighborhood was in an upbeat mood and elated with the moral advancement that had come to Elder Jackson's community. Many elderly people who were unable to walk great distances had a neighborhood church which they could attend. A few white people that lived in the community were delighted with the building of the new log church. A few had attended the school now they would be within walking distance of the new church.

Chapter Twenty-Three

Abraham was up at daybreak and hurried outside and took a few deep breaths as he looked up toward heaven. It was the second Sunday in May 1892. The roosters had stopped crowing as the sun slowly came up from behind the Eastern sky. When he came back inside Rilla observed how cheerful and pleasant he was.

"What's wrong Abram, Is today your birthday? You is mighty happy today."

"No, Rilla, today is the day we prepare to have our first service in our new church. Don't tell me you forgot."

"No, I ain't forgot, I just ain't seed you so happy. The chilun' have been seeing you too. Bill and General said they thought you had a fever or something."

Three hours later the narrow dirt road that led from all directions to the new church was teeming with men, women, and children. The majority walked while others came in wagons, buggies, and two-wheeled oxcarts. It was a time for everyone to sing and give praises to his or her God as they converged on the log church that sat upon the white sand hill close to the school. Soon the people would take their seats in the crowded sanctuary of the house of God. They had to build a brush arbor on the outside near the church to accommodate the large crowd of people.

The historic church had as many Caucasian church goers as they had African American. Many of Elder Jackson's fellow church members from Eden, Cedar Creek, Banks Creek, and other church people were there. The people were all on one accord and enjoyed the blessings that the God of Abraham, Isaac, and Jacob had granted unto them.

At the conclusion of the church service dinner was provided for everyone. Long tables were set and the people ate until they were full. And plenty of food was left for the people to take home. A few people remarked that the end of service was greater than its beginning because of all the food they had to eat.

At the end of the day of worship Abraham reminded George and Lewis that the church was built a little too small. They'd underestimated the number of people in the community that would attend the big meetings and special occasions.

Two months later in July 1892 George received word from the county officials that a railroad was to be built and it would encompass some of his land. He would have to give up a portion of his land for the railroad to be built. The Wadley Southern Railway would operate in the area and travel to distant points through Tattnall County and other counties in Southeast Georgia. George mentioned the building of the railroad to Abraham and Lewis so they'd be aware of what was to transpire.

Two weeks earlier, George purchased two hundred acres of land. This additional two hundred acres gave him a total of two hundred thirty-five acres. The additional land purchase joined Abraham's land to the West and East. George jokingly told his father that with the coming of the railroad through his property he'd no longer have to drive his horse and buggy long distances to church. He could ride the Wadley southern train to churches more than ten miles north of his residence.

Later that evening George and Benjamin were kidding Lewis about becoming a married man. Lewis was married to the pretty young woman he'd been seeing for four years.

"Hey, little brother, how does it feel to be married? I am happy for you. Let's see now, Benjamin and General is next; they'll be jumping the broom soon." George laughed.

"Wait a minute, George. Us Niggers don't jump over dem brooms anymore. De old Massa don't hab to give dere approval as they once did." Benjamin mischievously grinned.

"Ben I didn't know you could talk like the old slaves. Don't let papa hear you talk that way boy; he may disagree with you. If you know what I means."

It was near dusk dark and everyone had met at Abraham's house to go hunting. The summer weather was beautiful and they were looking forward to capturing the big cat that had terrorized everyone in the small community. For two weeks talk had spread throughout the community about seeing large size tracks of a wild animal. Rumors spread quickly that a black panther was loose in the woods killing deer and young calves. Two men fishing near the Ohoopee had reported to George that they'd actually seen a large catamount about six miles from Abraham's property.

"I believe it was the same cat that chased Bill and Millard. I heard them boys nearly tore down the door when they got home. But we's gwine to catch him tonight." Charles assured everyone.

"Yes, papa said they ran home through the woods and were nearly out of breath when they got to the door. Papa said he grabbed his shotgun as they banged on the door. He said he heard what sounded like an animal growl. He ran out the door and fired two shots in the direction of Tom." George said.

"No one told me anything about a cat chasing Bill and Millard. Papa or Mama didn't tell me anything about it." Benjamin said.

"Well George, We can use "Rabbit" to help us track down this cat."

"We're going to need more than "Rabbit" to help us get this cat. We don't have a trail to follow. But a good thing in our favor, is, it's not too dark tonight. We'll be able to see where we is going"

"Just what color is this cat? I heard he is black, as black as midnight; then I heard he is as brown as the October leaves. And how large is it?" General asked.

General pulled up behind George and whispered to him. "I saw some big cat tracks outside the chicken house yesterday. I told Benjamin and Dell; it looked like the cat Israel and Charles, and Henry were hunting."

The chase for the elusive animal continued for two hours and no one saw any signs or tracks that might lead them in the direction the cat traveled. They had only one dog leading the chase and it was George's slow-footed "Rabbit." George gave him that name because of his lack of speed for a hound dog. They continued their pursuit of the cat for another hour and there was no sign. After traveling in the thick woods for close to four hours a light rain began to fall. And the chase became more exciting as the men were unprepared for the rain; they began to grow uneasy and weary of the chase.

It was unusually quiet, only the sound of their footsteps against the leaves could be heard. An occasional sound of an owl and a night bird in the distance rattled their nerves as they continued the chase.

"Damn it! Here comes the rain. This is going to mess up our hunt." General yelled. What is we going do now?"

"Boy, getting upset, will only make things worse." George said in a calm voice. "We have to wait until "Rabbit" picks up his scent. "Rabbit" is slow, but we should hear something directly."

"More and likely his trail will be close to the Creek near old man Sikes place. Let's follow the winding creek." Lewis directed everyone to do.

Rabbit began to bark slowly as he moved about fifty yards further down near the creek. He abruptly stopped and began barking, looking up into a tall black gum tree. The large ferocious cat began growling, and "Rabbit" ran quickly back where George stood, howling and rubbing against George's left leg.

"A good thing it's not too dark tonight Bud." General told George gazing up into the tall black gum tree. "Is we still on papa's property or is this Mr. Sikes land?" Seconds later the sound of a thirty-thirty rifle burst in the air. The large catamount fell from the tree to the ground.

"Great shooting General Andrew Jackson." George and Lewis laughed. "Who taught you to shoot like that? I didn't know you could do it." George exclaimed. You got off four quick shots. How could you see?" You is got eagle eyes."

"He makes his own bullets too. Bet you ain't knowed that." Lewis shouted.

"Well Men, the hunt is finally over. I guess we'd better get on back home and see what else there is to do. I hoped the killing of this wild beast has fixed it so it won't kill any more chickens or kill any more young cows." George said with a sigh of relief.

The next week the news spread quickly of General's superb shooting and the killing of the catamount. It was said the big cat was the largest one every killed in the county. The demise of the predatory animal dispelled rumors that the crafty animal was attacking livestock in the northwestern part of the county. General earned the respect of his brothers as the best shot they'd ever seen.

Chapter Twenty-Four

The end of the school year program was postponed for nine days until the roof could be repaired. The children always had a school closing program to mark the end of the school year. The big day had parents and students rally for their favorite programs; events were scheduled for the inside and outside of the school building. The children participated in spelling contests, singing, dialogue, and dance contests. Outside the children participated in foot racing, high jump contests, sack racing, and horseshoe throwing. It was a jubilant occasion and a joyful day for everyone who attended.

The weather was nice and mild. The wind blew calmly against the tall pines; a flock of birds were seen flying high above against a clear blue sky. The indoor activities lasted for ninety minutes and the activities carried over to the outside. The foot racing activities occurred first; followed by the high jump activities, the potato sack race, and then the horse shoe contest.

The events lasted close to four hours. Everyone got a chance to meet the children's teachers and everyone who attended the school closing program. Sometimes the events carried over until night. But this year careful planning and hard work on everyone's part assured for a timely order of events.

A few of the older men and women were present at the school closing event. Loance, Charlotte, George, Nellie, Jacob, Henry,

Israel, and Macy were all present. George recalled his first Thanksgiving Day and school opening dinner. It was here, thirteen years earlier that he'd gone hunting with his dog "Rabbit." He disclosed how his dog received the name "Rabbit." It was here on the white sand hill; he remembered how Mr. Fraser had talked to the children about the importance of an education. And in exhilaration he remembered Nellie's demeanor and behavior.

She was a beautiful young lady, with large brown eyes and long black hair. George thought to himself, "I know you ain't marrying any Indian girl. Is you George?"

"Some peoples say the buckra don't want us to have a school 'cause they is afraid of us. That can't be true 'cause some of the buckra children go to school here. The first thing I learned to do was read the Bible. Befo' I learnt to write my name, I learnt to read the Bible. When you learns to read and write, your mind wanders and you get ideas 'bout who you is, and what you can become." He recalled Loance's words.

Before everyone was ready to leave the festivities of the day a strange gentlemen came on the school grounds looking for the owner of a large black mule. He said that was his mule and it was stolen by someone at the school. The man had a vicious look on his face and carried a cowhide whip in his right hand. He wore a large rim brown hat, and was dressed in a red plaid shirt, and had a pair of black string up boots that were united at the top.

"Go get General." George whispered to Bill. "Hurry up, tell him to come quickly."

Minutes later General was on the school grounds where the disturbance took place. He saw the man who'd caused the confusion and distraction. He walked over to where the man stood: "Boy you have five seconds to leave Jackson Town. Move, move out, three of your seconds is already gone." General pulled his forty-four from his right pocket and shot twice in the air; the man ran away without looking back.

The people went away in awe wondering what had happened. The large black mule belonged to Lewis. Lewis had the mule for two weeks and didn't tell anyone he'd purchased the handsome animal. He was working with Abraham at the time checking fence that had fallen down. Abraham had heard that it was possible for a rainstorm to come their way and the downpour could be heavy. Abraham told Lewis, he felt it in his bones that it may rain. He and Lewis missed all the excitement that happened.

The next day George and Lewis came to Abraham with exciting news. "You tell him first, Lewis." George said. No, George you're the oldest, you go first."

"What's all this about. You go first. No, you are the oldest, you tell him. Tell me what. Abraham asked.

"Papa, since I'm the oldest, I'll go first. Did you know that General has been married since August 1891?" George said in disbelief.

"Okay, Lewis. What's your surprise?"

"Papa, I was going to tell you the same thing."

"He told me last year he wanted to get married and I told him if that was what he wanted to move ahead. That's why he wanted to move in the little house on the side the main road."

"Papa, don't tell me Benjamin is married too."

"George, what about your newborn baby; how is he? What is his name?"

"His name is Ira. How many acres of land do you have now?"

"Altogether, papa, I have two hundred and thirty five acres. I'm only thirty-two papa.

"What about you Lewis? How many acres of land do you have?"

"Papa, I have one hundred thirty acres; and I'm only twenty nine." Lewis gestured, tipping his hat.

Chapter Twenty-Five

Two years later in 1894 Jackson Town was growing as well as changing. The Wadley Southern Train was now making trips from Darien to Wadley and Elder Jackson rode the train to all of his church meetings out of the county. He made trips as well to the far Northern end of the county. George had two sons Elza and Ira.

Nellie and George enjoyed living on their two hundred thirty-five acre farm. The large log house was surrounded by tall pines and rail fences; peach, plum, pear, pecan, and wild cherry trees encompassed the land. The Wadley Southern Railroad lay to the east and Northeast of their farm.

It was time for the annual frolic to take place on the Abraham Jackson place in Jackson Town. Each year it took place in the month of July to coincide with their youngest son's birthday. The event took place every July 22nd and all family members were expected to attend. This was the first celebration of its kind and everyone was excited; and Rilla and Abraham were animated. Early that morning they began preparing food for the celebration.

"Bill have you been feeding those chickens?" Rilla asked.

"Yes mama I sure have."

"I don't know Bud, those chickens look a might poor. I can see all of their bones; boy, what you been feeding those poor birds?"

"What happened to all my eggs in the hen house? No Bill you don't let the foxes into the chicken house to gather eggs and they don't pay you. And don't tell me Babe was 'spose to gather the eggs either."

The July sun beamed down on the historic community like a fiery furnace. The sun shone brightly over the Eastern sky and had the making of a sultry, but beautiful day for a frolic. All of Abraham and Rilla's grown children had promised to attend the celebration this day. Abraham had to make sure their celebration did not violate his Christian principles. He had assured everyone before it inception that he gave his staunch approval of it. The feast carried with it a busy work schedule as well.

"Mama, did you know that Della has a boyfriend?"

"No, I didn't child, who is this boyfriend of hers?"

"I heard his papa got a large farm."

"Nancy, I don't have time for jokes today. Come on we've got lots of work to do."

"I heard he comes from North Carolina," Nancy laughed.

"How can you get rich picking cotton? Don't try and fool me child. How do you know so much about Dell's boyfriend?"

"Let's talk about something else. Is General here? He promised to take care of everything."

"Bill, come here. I need three more chickens. Go and catch me three chickens; tell Babe to help you."

"Mama, bill doesn't like to catch chickens." Idella laughed.

"But he is the first one at the table when it's time to eat. You know what he is saying."

"What foolishness does you girls have up your sleeves now?"

"Tell her Nancy, what Bill is been saying."

"Mama, Nancy says when papa is saying the grace, Bill doesn't close his eyes. He gets as much food as he can before papa finish blessing the food."

"And that's funny. I am gwine to skin that boy alive." Rilla shouted.

The time was winding down for everyone to be in place and working on their assigned tasks. Each person knew what he or she was assigned to do. Rilla was uneasy and grew impatient awaiting General's arrival. A large gathering of relatives and friends was expected and she wanted to be prepared.

"Where is that General. He said he would be on time. He is supposed to get that wash pot ready and the fire heating the water." Rilla mumbled.

"You got plenty of time Mama. We ain't gwine to kill hogs; General will be here."

"Who said that?"

"I did Mama."

"Is that you Lewis?"

"No, Mama, Lewis isn't your oldest son. I, King George is your oldest son."

The family enjoyed each other's company and the exchanging of tales and stories. Everyone missed Abraham Jr. they hadn't heard from or seen him in five years. His father began to worry about his whereabouts. His non presence reminded Abraham of his separation from his mother and brothers during slavery. Everyone had been waiting for days and weeks with hope that Abraham Jr. would return.

"Papa said he wanted that big red rooster for dinner the next second Sunday. Did you hear me Bill? Nancy, you and Amanda can help him clean that old rooster. You chilun' be careful and don't let him stick his spurs in you. We is all in too big of a hurry. Let's settle down."

Talk still circulated in the community about General's perfect shots that brought down the large catamount in the area. George still agreed that he'd never seen anyone shoot so straight. He'd seen his father shoot at still objects, but not at a moving target as his brother General did. He was saluted for his act of courage at the school closing program when he intervened to disarm an intruder with no weapon, just the words from his mouth. Talk spread rapidly in the small community and in the Northern end of the county; twenty-year old General was a hero in the community.

Amanda and Nancy were to keep tract of everyone who was scheduled to come to the joyous celebration. "Tina, Harriet, and Macy Ann, is in charge of the gossip." Nancy whispered in a joyful manner.

"About how many will be coming Amanda," Babe asked.

"I know mama who is coming."

"I thought you was helping General make the molasses water."

"Benjamin said he would help him, mama. George and his children is coming; Macy Ann and Israel; I don't know if they have any children coming. Continue to count—Harriet, Charles and James is coming; Mr Loance and Mrs. Charlotte; Papa's white friends—he have 'bout ten of them and don't forget three white preachers may come also. They like to call papa and George Uncle Abram and Uncle George."

"Is you sure that's everybody Babe? And you didn't leave any of the chilun' out."

"No, Mama, that's everybody. Mama you is talking too fast and in too big of a hurry; slow down. Babe chuckled, placing his hand on her shoulder.

The entire day went well and everyone arrived on time to take part in the first celebration of the youngest son's commemorative birthday festivity that would bring good luck and blessings upon the family. The children and grandchildren were responsible for the organizing and carrying into fruition the celebration. Some of the family members were divided over the words feast, frolic, and celebration. Only a few people understood what they called those big words.

One of Elder Jackson's friend's from Eden said a few words to wish the people well and for them to have a joyous return home. "De good Lord sends his rain to fall on de jest and de unjest alike. Isn't that what He says Elder Jackson. And He sends His sun to shine on de good and on de evil."

Chapter Twenty-Six

It was September 12, 1895 and Booker T. Washington came to Atlanta to give his famous Cotton States Exposition speech before a predominantly mostly white vacillating audience. He was a former slave as Abraham was and now the founder of Tuskegee Institute in Alabama. The speech set the tone for race relations and racial progress between African Americans and Caucasians in the south and the nation. Mr. Washington wasn't an advocate for social equality among the races in the south, Georgia, or the United States. His speech did more to cause division among the races than it did to bring social unity.

1895 was the year in which Abraham applied a second time for a pension from the United States Army as an invalid soldier. His shoulder injury prevented him from fully doing the manual farm labor he was able to do prior to his enlistment in the Union Army. Upon his enlistment in the army as a volunteer soldier he received no bounty for his enlistment. He first applied in January 1893 and again in April of 1895.

Loance Eason, George and Harriet's father-in-law died two months before Booker T. Washington's infamous Altanta Compromise Speech. The family was celebrating Independence Day, when the seventy-five year old patriot of Tattnall County passed. Nellie, George, Harriet, and Charles along with his wife

Charlotte were present when he expired. Loance never gave up hope; he remained dedicated and upbeat about the progress being made by African Americans in his community. He continued working on his two hundred seventy-five acre farm until his health failed him. He had two large horses and two wonderful mules; a large surrey buggy and two colossal two horse wagons.

He was a jovial person and seemed happy to be around. He was talkative and never at a loss for words. He enjoyed working on his large farm and attending to his horses and other farm animals. He enjoyed crowds and mixing with people. During Reconstruction he worked with the political leaders along with Elder Jackson and a few of the other local African American leaders during this rebuilding process in local and in state history.

George spoke to Abraham after Loances's funeral: "Papa he reminded me of you before he died. I always wanted to be able to read and write. I wanted to know what it means to feel like a human being and not an animal. Human beings have feelings different from animals. One bad thing I didn't like about slavery, don't get me wrong, I hated everything about slavery. But one terrible thing, no human being should be sold away from his parents, never to see them again."

"Papa when I talked to him, he had such a solemn look on his face. I saw tears come down both eyes. I cried myself. Mrs. Eason wanted to know what we was crying about."

"George, what's going to happen to his farm?" Abraham asked.

"I don't know what Charles and them is going to do. This white man, Mr. Woods I heard is going to be the administrator. You know what happens when they get hold to your land."

"Mrs. Charlotte is got to sign some papers. But she can't read or write, someone has got to help her. Papa, I'm glad you built that school. And I hope more colored people learn to read and write."

George's Third son was born in January 1895. He and Nellie named him Lester; he was born six months before the death of his maternal grandfather Loance. Elza was sixteen and Ida was seven. General had a son born in 1892, his first child Harmon; Lewis and Ann Jane had a son Newton, born in 1894. The Extended family of Abraham and Rilla was growing larger as their children were married and moved on.

William T. Atkinson was elected governor of Georgia a year earlier in October 1894 and the political wheels of Jim Crow law began to grind slowly; the move toward political disfranchisement of African Americans began to affect their lives. The southern states had already begun a move to make the African American voter a non political entity.

A year later in 1896 the United States Supreme Court handed down the Plessy decision which established the basis of "Separate but Equal" practices in the United States and laid the foundation for legal segregation. The decision first applied to segregated railway cars for African Americans and Caucasians. The infamous decision paved the way for legal segregation in public schools, parks, hotels, restaurants, theatres, and in all walks of public life in the South and in the United states.

These laws didn't break the progress and determination of Abraham and his growing family in their quest to move forward. They continued to grow and make progress at the log school and the membership increased at the log church. Two white children continued to attend the school and many more Caucasians participated in worship service. Abraham, George, and now Lewis were landowners and the trio remained vigilant in checking their land titles at the courthouse. This tireless checking assured them of the proper recording of their land titles.

The railroad was in dire need of cross-ties and men to provide the necessary labor for the railroad to function. The people were jubilant and excited to have another means of transportation in the area. They had waited a long time for transportation by train from Darien to Wadley. Before the building of Wadley Southern,

Abraham and George relied mainly on horse and buggy to travel to places of great distance. General was among the first workers hired to hew trees into cross-ties for the railroad. General at twenty-one years of age stood six feet-six inches tall. He was rugged and suited for the hard work involved in cutting of trees.

Employers appointed to hire men to cut cross-ties went from house to house in the small communities and towns. They hired laborers to do the rough work which required strong able-bodied men. The conditions were bad under which the men labored; snakes and insects, as well as a nature itself, when the heavy rain flooded the roads and trails.

"General, are you going to work today, we are already late." The wagon on which the men rode moved slowly and the wheels squeaked. "We should've been in the woods by now." Marshall grumbled.

"I told you boys I don't work on Mondays. That's my time to check my farm tools." General declared leaning down as he stepped outside.

"That'll be fine General. I was just checking. What about tomorrow, same time."

"Tomorrow will be the day, I'll be here."

Abraham gave General ten acres of land for the planting of cotton and corn. He had a fine mule. The first mule he bought died five days later. He thought someone had poisoned him. Abraham thought his mule showed symptoms of being poisoned. Lewis, George, and Benjamin had helped General with the mule he had. His two brothers pitched in to help. They gave him a plough, shovel, two hoes.

"General this will help you some to get started. I heard you are going to help Mr. Morris cut cross-ties on tomorrow. I wish you luck little brother." George said looking up at General, smiling.

Later that evening, George was at Abraham and Rilla's where he met Millard and Bill. Harriet, Macy and Tina were there as well.

"I see all my sisters are here. Do they live here mama? Every time I come by they are here." I got some work for you three to do if you don't have any."

"Nah suh Massa, us is tired of worken, us ain't got pade from de last hundred years work." Harriet said bursting with laughter.

"Who are you three joking about? I've got to go, mama where is papa?

"I remembered her mama. She was short and fat. She had two teeth in her mouth"

"No Harriet, she had two teeth in the bottom of her mouth. I knew her well. She was that buckra man's woman." Macy said looking at Harriet.

"Don't let the preacher hear y'all talking like that. Harriet chuckled.

The morning air was hot and humid. The sky was clear and blue; there was not a cloud to be seen in it. A mild breeze blew slowly from the East toward the west. The serene wind regulated the temperature as the air began to cool. Vultures flew in a circle high above the tall pines. Their presence usually signaled something in the area had died. George and Elza had been plowing corn all morning; mostly Elza because George was in and out. It was twelve noon and they stopped for a lunch break.

"How is that husband of yours Harriet?"

"Who is you talking 'bout Charles?"

"Yes, you got moe than one."

"Charles is helping mama Charlotte take care of some business. They are trying to keep the buckra from taking their land."

"I'm so glad Papa Loance did learn to read the Bible and write his name. That was all he talked about. And don't forget he enjoyed talking about those beautiful horses and them two old mules." Harriet grinned.

There were rumors that Charlotte's grandmother was of Cherokee Indian ancestry. Talk was that she was on the infamous

"Trail of Tears. It was said that was where Nellie got her beautiful skin and her long black hair. But Loance dispelled such supposition as idle gossip; he often told George such unverified information violated sound reasoning. Loance himself had heard of the Cherokee Indians having to leave North Georgia when gold was discovered in the mountains near Dahlonega. He argued that his wife's grandmother was not of Indian ancestry and such a place didn't interest him. He proclaimed his wife's grandmother was sold into Georgia from South Carolina.

A few Indians lived in the county and adjoining counties but his wife's grandmother was not one of them. An Indian worked for Abraham on his farm in the late 1880s and George knew him to be a hard worker helping to plow Abraham's old mule. But he worked for one year and then left. No one knew when he left or where he went, he wasn't heard from again.

Chapter Twenty-Seven

Both African Americans and Caucasians were fascinated about being in the company of first, Abraham and later George. In the late 1870s and 1880s they enjoyed being in the company of Abraham whom the whites called "Uncle Abram," and later George, whom they grew found of and referred to him as "Uncle George." George was the benefactor of several who came to him for help. One white man lived on his farm in a little building near the flat woods. Everyone, who suffered from a lack of finances and the needy came to him for help or assistance.

Beginning early in 1894, a Caucasian woman who knew George when he was a five year old slave wanted to help teach him the alphabet and how to write his name. She remembered him when he became a man and acquired a large tract of land. She was impressed with his hard work and the progress he made when he became an adult. She desired to help him attain a legal knowledge of how the court system worked. She was known to him as Miss Kate. She wanted George to learn as much legal information as possible in regards to land and land titles.

"George, whenever we are going to have court, I'll drop you a line or two and let you know. I want you to come and see what's going on, so you can see how the law operates.

"Now, don't forget, Uncle George, whenever we are going to have court, I'll drop you a line or two and let you know before the court date. I want you to come and learn about our laws and how they operate."

A week later, George received a letter from Miss Kate reminding him of the time and court date. The day of court he left early in the morning against a mild lazy wind that blew in from the North toward the South. He hitched "Brownie" to his buggy and was ready to travel an hour later. The town of Reidsville was ten miles from his house. He could easily make the journey in less than two hours. It was a cool spring day. Rail fences lined the landscape on both sides of the narrow dusty road. A half-mile down the road he had to pass over a shallow stream about twenty yards long and one foot deep. Two rabbits ran through an opening in the fence and scurried down the road; then abruptly stopped and ran into the woods.

George always rode in the buggy with his left foot hanging down to the side. Big Brownie came to a stop at George's command. He looked around and heard a dog barking. To his surprise it was "Rabbit." He climbed from the buggy to remove a large limb that had fallen in the road the night before. "Rabbit, you can't come with me today. You is got to go back home. I've got business to attend to. Move on! Go on back. "Rabbit" turned around and ran back barking as if he was chasing a rabbit. George removed the limb from the road and was on his way to observe the court proceedings.

He arrived at the courthouse in ample time before the start of the court session. He saw Kate waiting outside to meet him. He found a hitching post for "Brownie." He and Kate exchanged greetings and strolled inside the courthouse to await the start of the judicial process. Kate made known to George that when court recessed for lunch she would place him in line with the others and walk to the hotel cafeteria for lunch. All eyes were fastened on George. A few white people thought he was Kate's servant. A distinguished looking white-haired gentleman of the county who lived in the new town of Collins recognized George.

"Hello, Uncle George, how are you today?"

"I'll do. just common thank you."

"I'm surprised to see you today. Uncle, how many children do you have now? I heard you and your wife had a baby boy this past January."

Yes, Mr. Holland, that's right. I have four children; two boys and two girls."

Some whites in the hotel cafeteria resented a black man in their presence and sat far away from where George dined alone. The majority of whites recognized him as Elder Abraham Jackson oldest son and they knew Elder Jackson to be an honorable man. Like his son, George, Abraham owned three hundred acres of land in the county. He and George were frequently seen at the courthouse checking on their land titles.

After lunch George returned to court to learn all he could about the problems involved in the acquisition of land and land titles. He knew one thing about land and that was to keep his taxes paid on his land. This he learned early from his father. Abraham was an active participant in the registering of African American voters during the early years of Reconstruction in the county. In 1876 he was accused of not paying his taxes on his three hundred acres of land and almost lost it.

Court adjourned at four O' clock and George hurriedly left the wooden building unhitched his horse, "Brownie" and returned to Jackson Town. Half-way between his home and the new town of Collins he gave his horse a thirty-minute rest as was his usual practice. He wanted to arrive home before dark and to check on his children. In his absence he knew he could depend on Elza to take care of things until he returned. Nellie had her hands full with her three young children. He was happy to return to his farm and was impressed with the things he had seen and heard in court. He found most of the white people friendly and helpful during the proceedings.

A year passed since Abraham first applied for his military pension. His friend Luke questioned him why it had taken him so long to apply for his pension. He enlightened Abraham that his injury was in the line of duty and he was entitled to a pension because of his injury. The injury to his shoulder had prevented him from doing strenuous farm work. His friend Jack made known to Abraham that he would attest to the fact in writing if he needed him to do so.

Two days after listening to the advice of his friends Abraham decided to take a trip to the post office to see if he'd received any mail from the Military Pension Bureau. The day began as a beautiful warm morning; Abraham hitched Skipper to his buggy and drove to the little post office three miles away. He rode in his buggy to the post office each Wednesday to check on his mail. He hitched his horse to the hitch provided for the people who drove horses and buggies or horses and wagons. The great majority of the people had horses and mules. But Abraham enjoyed driving his horse Skipper to the post office. Skipper was now fifteen years of age and that was old for a horse or mule.

Abraham walked over to the small building to greet the man who worked in the post office.

"How are you doing today Uncle Abraham," he said as he grimaced.

"Just common, Mr. Buddy. Do you have any good news for me? Skipper is growing tired of making blink trips."

"No Uncle, I ain't got anything for you yet. You know how slow the Yankee government is. You know, Uncle Abram, you are the only colored man around here that was injured during the late war."

"I don't rightly know, Mr. Buddy. I know of ten men that were in the war, but I don't know any of their business." Abraham commented, void of a smile. "I'll see you again next Wednesday." Elder Jackson saluted the postman as he left.

Chapter Twenty-Eight

The beginning of a new century ushered in many changes that the state and nation hadn't seen in the nineteenth century. The United States Supreme Court handed down the Plessy v. Ferguson decision in 1896 which made segregation the law of the land. The infamous decision laid down the doctrine of "Separate but Equal." Segregation of the two races was legal as long as African Americans had equal facilities with Caucasians in theaters, hotels, public transportation, parks, and other public places. The Plessey decision was a disappointment for African Americans because the two races drifted further and further apart. The underlying result meant racial isolation and unequal treatment in all aspect of social, economic, and political life for the African American race.

The new century saw the United States become a world power. The Spanish American War gave the United States new acquisitions of territory as a result of the war. The nation acquired the Philippine Islands, Hawaii, and Puerto Rico. And Cuba gained its Independence from Spain. African American soldiers participated in this war and help to lead the charge up San Juan Hill alongside Teddy Roosevelt and his "Rough Riders."

At the start of the new century George had Four young children, Ira aged eight; Lester five; Lilla three and Ethel one. Lewis had two young boys; Newton age five and Lonnie age three.

Destitute people in the community both Black and Whites came to George and Abraham for help; both humanitarian and charitable assistance. Father and son were compassionate. The two men were warmhearted and sympathetic to the needs and concerns of their less fortunate neighbors. For food they invited the poor to gather vegetables from their gardens and fruit from their fruit trees.

As part of the Reconstruction occupation army in the military district of Savannah and Augusta in Georgia; and Hamburg and Charleston in South Carolina, Abraham told of the pain and suffering he saw as a direct result of the war.

The middle of January 1900 George remembered the words of Miss Kate as he prepared to return to the courthouse five years later. "Don't worry, Uncle George I'll make sure you are treated just like all the rest of us." Those words echoed in the back of his mind on a cold winter morning as he prepared to take the ten mile trip to the courthouse. He was one of a handful of African American men in the county to have a fine horse and buggy. The narrow road that led to the courthouse was rough and bumpy. Mud clogged the buggy wheels as the road dried out from a cold rain that had fallen two days earlier. George wore his heavy black coat to keep him warm and a hat on his head to protect his ears from the chilly air.

Upon his arrival at the courthouse he saw an elderly African American man standing begging for food. This was a strange sight for him because he's never seen anyone near the courthouse begging for food or anything else. The man was bareheaded and had on a raggedy long sleeved plain cotton shirt. George hitched his horse to the hitching post and immediately came to where the man stood to see if he could be of any help. The man petitioned George for food. He gave the man what looked like a silver dollar. The beggar was so happy to receive the gift that he left in such a hurry he forgot to thank George for the money.

Later, he observed the court proceedings for the morning and had to leave before he got a chance to talk to Miss Kate. He needed to return home and check with twenty-one year old Elza and Nellie about his cows that had been climbing over his rail fences. He had twelve cows and fifteen hogs and they were anxious at times to test the strength of the fence to see if they could break out. Elza had repaired all the fences so none of the animals could break out and wander away.

As he returned home and drove "Brownie" to the barn and unhitched him. He was surprised to see Mrs. Lizzie Tillman outside his house talking to Nellie and Ida. The weather had warmed up considerably, but it was still cold. Nellie had a fire burning under her large wash pot and clothes were boiling in it.

"Mr. George, I'm glad to see you." Lizzie was a dignified and self-respecting woman.

"Good afternoon, Mrs. Tillman. I'm surprised to see you here." A mild wind blew across the landscape, but the air was calm as the sparks from the fire died down.

"Mr. Jackson, we need to borrow some sweet potatoes and a little sausage from you. My husband has been sick for four weeks. He hurt his back when the wagon fell on him. I pray every night Mr. George that God will watch over us and help us." Before her husband's accident she helped Nellie with her children during the birth of both Ira and Lester.

"Mrs. Lizzie I will have Elza to go to the crib and get you some sweet potatoes and syrup; and Nellie will get you some sausage from the smokehouse. "Stop by papa's and see if he has sometin' for you." I'm sure he'll have something to give you."

"God bless you and Miss Nellie. I thank y'all for everything."

Four months later, in May the children looked forward to the close of another school term. The school year lasted for five months. Forty children were enrolled in the school in 1900. The weather was warm and the children enjoyed the activities associated with the end of the school term. As usual, the children were involved with activities on the inside which included spelling contests, dialogue, recitation of time tables, and memorization of Bible verses. Later the outside activities covered running, high jump, sack potato race, and horse shoe pitching. The children were excited about all the activities and everyone participated. Their teacher Mrs. Jane Terry worked hard all week to prepare her pupils for this special day.

An hour after the festivities were over and everyone had eaten dinner a disturbance occurred in front of the school building. A tall thin rugged looking man entered the school grounds. He walked with a limp; his right leg appeared to be shorter than his left. He was upset and adamant. His wife had run away with one of the share croppers in the area and he was going to release his frustrations on someone at the school closing event. He appeared to be heavily intoxicated. The inebriated man waved a small caliber pistol in his right hand. The children and their parents scattered in all directions to extricate themselves from the enthralled tenant farmer.

The word of the turmoil hurriedly reached General who was less than a hundred yards away. He was resting, taking a break from his travel to the southern part of the county. Pressed for time himself, he quickly rushed to the scene of the disturbance. General was faced with a similar challenge at a school closing five years earlier. In five minutes he was at the school. Except for the cursing and vulgarity coming from the mouth of the dispirited man, total silence surrounded the historic school. General walked slowly toward the tall thin man who'd frightened everyone into the one room school building.

"Boy, are you lost?" General asked the man in a voice just above a whisper. The tall lean man flinched, as he took one step backward.

"Can't a man have a little fun? I jest want to learn the alphabet and learn how to write my name." The man laughed as he staggered forward, the pistol still in his right hand.

"Boy, you've got five minutes to sober up and leave Jackson Town. Three of your minutes have already passed." General reached his hand in his pocket and pulled out his forty-four and shot in the air three times. The man saw the size of General's pistol and began to run; he fell down, and hurriedly got up and limped hastily down the hill to the main road.

Thirty minutes later, everyone returned to their regular school closing activities. Miss Terry invited General to stay on and observe the activities for the rest of the day. But he had to return to his work for the remainder of the day. The children and their parents were overjoyed that the morally depraved man who'd interrupted their activities had been removed from the school grounds. This was the second time the school activities had been interrupted by an individual not associated with the school closing. Whenever trouble interrupted the normal school day or school closing George, Abraham, and Lewis could always trust that General would be close by.

Chapter Twenty-Nine

George yearned to progress and keep in tune with new ideas and learn new farming techniques. He wanted to move beyond the nineteenth century and keep abreast with the changes that the new century ushered in. He remembered the rough times in the early 1890s. His father Elder Abraham Jackson was growing older and he wanted to help him supervise his farm and farmland. Lewis was beginning to prosper as a farmer. He had increased his cotton acreage and corn that was grown. The three of them had close to seven hundred acres of land. George reminded his father that he wanted to farm more effectively and efficiently.

Times were growing more difficult in the county for African American farmers. The three men remembered the rhetoric and insincerity of Tom Watson who played politics with both the African American farmers and the white farmers. Abraham warned his two oldest sons about the political rhetoric of the Democratic Party and the new Populist Party and its leaders. They were hit hard by the Panic of 1893, which didn't make matters better for African Americans in the county.

"Papa, we've got to have the right tools on the farm to become better farmers. We have got to depend on more than cotton as our main money crop. We have got cows, hogs, and we have timber. We are all doing well with our vegetable gardens. You've got to get Millard and Bill to work harder if they are going to have something."

"I know Bud. We have got to have more tools than an axe, picks, shovels, and the like to help us become better farmers. I have been telling your Uncle Frank. I told him he could work his farm and still learn to read and write."

"What do you think about that Uncle Frank?" George relented. Those old buckra will let everyone know if you can read and write."

"That's mostly what I preach to my congregation on Sundays. I beg them to get an education. They don't need a fancy education; just learn the simple elements of sixth grade learning. I agreed with Booker T. Washington in some respects. You can learn to farm and use your hands as well as read poetry."

"Mr. Abraham, I was almost wiped out of farming by this so called Panic of 1893." Frank fussed.

"I am older than all of you. When we were in chains and had shackles around our ankles—slave law denied us the right to be a man; denied us the right to be human; the law said we were three-fifths of the buckra man. We were in the same class as their cattle, hogs, mules, and dogs." Abraham growled. "I once swore that no buckra people were going to heaven. But now I preach in the buckra churches and a lot of my friends are white."

"Elza tells me they got a new school in Savannah for colored people. They call it Georgia State Industrial College. Yes, a new college for Coloreds, whatever that is. That's what Mr. Booker T. Washington was talking about in Atlanta back in 1895. But he didn't say anything 'bout colored people going to college." George said.

"I doesn't need to go all the way to uh—what's dat place called, uh—in Savannah to learn how to plow and 'bout farming. I knows how to plant corn and cotton. I jest wants to learn how to write my name and how to read de Bible 'befo I passes on."

George thought it was useless talking to his uncle about how to improve as a farmer. "Don't you want to learn new ideas and how to make your land produce more per acre? Don't you want to make progress Uncle Frank? What about your children and grandchildren, don't you want them to have an education?"

"What about you George, do you have an eddication?" Frank asked.

Two years later, illiteracy and a lackadaisical attitude with regard to an education continued to plague the African American community. The number of tenant farmers in the county continued to be far reaching as the number of African American farms continued to decline. The era of good feelings among the races was on a downward spiral. The Plessey decision rendered by the United Supreme Court six years earlier continued to have a polarizing effect on the African American in his quest for political and economic justice. The push for the spread of Jim Crow laws and the disenfranchisement of the African American voter continued to take center stage as the number one issue for those who called for the demise of the African American landowner. Abraham contemplated whether our state and nation had abandoned its Christian values and practices as a nation founded upon the noble ideal that "all men are created equal" written in the Declaration of Independence. And the words enshrined in its preamble to the United States Constitution and the pledge to its flag "indivisible with liberty and justice for all."

Chapter Thirty

It was January 1904 and Nellie was expecting her sixth child to be born in June. She and George were happy and had planned a train ride to savannah as soon as the baby was born. George had promised her that he'd take her to Georgia's oldest city. He heard his father talk about Savannah when he was stationed there for three months during the Civil War.

"What I'm going to do Nell is talk to Lewis to see if he and Jane want to go with us after the baby is born." George said.

"I spoke to Harriet about that pretty red dress I saw in that catalog. And Harriet likes it, and says she is going to get Charles to buy her one."

"Wasn't Papa Abraham in Savannah when President Lincoln was kilt? Did he like Savannah?" Nellie asked.

"Let's talk about something else. I am King George and you are Queen Nellie. We'll go after the baby is born. But we don't know when that'll be. But I am going to buy you two red dresses." George said pointing to Nellie's stomach.

"Don't do that; it's bad luck. It's bad luck to do that before the baby is born."

"Who told you that? Is that Indian talk? No such thing; I don't believe that."

The weather was cold and George and Elza had to put up a fence before the day was over. Ira was twelve years of age and beginning to help on the large farm. He was large enough to make sure the animals were properly fed and given water to drink. George and Elza had been working on the fence for two weeks. They didn't get much work done because of the extremely cold weather. George looked for it to snow. He remembered the large snowfall five years earlier in 1899. A large snow fell that winter and stayed on the ground for one week before it melted. The snow that year blanketed in the entire state. Frost was on the ground each morning and didn't melt until three or four hours after the sun arose.

Five months later on June 21, 1904 Nellie became gravely ill. Harriet attempted to cheer her up talking about her nine year old son.

"Nellie I remember when the child was born. I think it snowed that day. No I think it was 'spose to snow that night and it didn't. Wake up Nell. Don't fall asleep on me. That boy Les looks just like his grandpa Papa Loance.

"I heard what you said Harriet. You said Les looks just like Papa." Nellie said coughing as she sat up in the bed.

"Come to think of it, Nellie he does favor his grandpapa Loance. The way he walks and the way he even grins like papa Loance. Come here Lester, let me see you walk." Harriet laughed.

Later that night Nellie died peacefully. She gave birth to a baby boy whom she and George named James. The baby survived as the small newborn was delivered by the sixty year old midwife. The children, except for Elza were asleep. Nellie's death was a shock to everyone who knew her. It was a sad occasion for George and his five children. He talked to his mother just two days before her death. He recalled how well she looked.

He had promised her that as soon as the baby was born they were going to take a trip to Savannah on the train.

"Mama, I had promised her that I was going to buy her that red dress she wanted. Lewis and Ann were going with us. It's hard to love someone and then have them leave you. But the good Lord knows best. She was so young mama; we were only married twenty-five years."

"Don't worry son, she is in a better place now. You know, I knowed something was wrong the other day, when I heard all of them old birds uh singing. They was flying all over the place. Son, I saw red birds, blue birds, and brown birds. I even saw woodpeckers and I heard them pecking in that big oak tree. An old redbird even flew inside the house and fell against the window. My mama told me her mama saw an old crow fly into her cabin one night; and that was nothing but an omen. The next night her papa was hanged by the paddy rollers. "That was way back in 1819, five months befo' yo 'grandma was born."

"Mama she was too young to die; Nell was only forty-two. But the good book tells us there is a time to die and there is a time to be born. James was born and Nellie died. There is a time to cry and there is a time to laugh." He broke down and wept with his mother by his side.

George wanted to have seven sons like his father Abraham. He'd been told the number seven was a lucky number. He always wanted to be like his father. He saw in him the character he wanted to instill in his sons. He observed that few men in the county exhibited the attributes of Abraham in character, courage, or temperament.

Early the next day Abraham came over to George's to console him and offer him solace. He briefly talked to the sheriff who came by to offer his sympathy to George. Minutes later, General rode up in his wagon pulled by his big black mule who he called David. He heard the sheriff speak to his father and he was curious as to what was said.

"Good morning preacher, I'm sorry to hear of the death of Uncle George's wife. I've known aunt Nellie since 1889, close to fifteen years."

George met the sheriff just outside the door before Abraham got a chance to invite him inside the house. He had known Sheriff Kennedy for twenty years. They often crossed paths at the courthouse when court was in session and sometimes when he was checking his land titles. General observed the conversation between Abraham, George, and Sheriff Kennedy. He had his thirty-thirty Winchester in his wagon in case there was a dispute that needed to be settled. The Sheriff had heard of General's reputation with a gun. He'd heard of the two incidents that happened at the colored school closing activities. The word spread quickly about General's involvement in the two disturbances.

At sixteen, Ida was George and Nellie's oldest daughter. The lot fell upon her to help take care of the three youngest children along with her newborn baby brother. Ida was sixteen and almost grown. She was a bright student at the school on the white sand hill. She excelled in reading, writing, spelling and arithmetic. Abraham bragged to George and Nellie that Ida would be the next teacher at the school. She got along well with her siblings and cousins.

Shortly after Abraham and General left, Benjamin came over to pay his respects to George and his children. Benjamin was thirty-two years of age and married. "I'm sorry George to hear, I didn't know. I just heard yesterday." Ben said looking up at a large picture of Nellie hanging on the wall. Harriet told me about your lost earlier this morning."

George was surrounded by his children and Harriet, Macy, Lewis and Ann Jane. Charles, William, and Millard came a half hour later. George's friend Kate came to offer her condolences after learning of Nellie's premature death. She brought her friend Alice along with her in her buggy.

"Uncle George. I'm sure going to miss aunt Nellie." Kate said in a quiet manner. "Yes, her fried chicken and sweet potato pie was the best I ever tasted. Did she have a recipe for those pies she baked or did she do it from memory. I meant to ask her, but never got around to it.

"She could sew too. She made some of the prettiest dresses I have ever seen. I understand how you feel Uncle. I know you're going to miss her."

"Yes, Miss Kate I truly miss her. I'd be lying if I didn't; especially late in the evening and at night. I miss her calling me to come to supper and making sure the children didn't stay up too late." George showed sympathy for his deceased wife.

After seven days of mourning, Nellie Eason Jackson's funeral was held at Bethaven Primitive Baptist Church on a warm summer day. Springtime had given way to summer just a few days before. The grass was green and the church was surrounded by beautiful red, white, and pink wildflowers. Spring had left its beautiful signature on nature's gifts to mankind as a reminder of life's renewal process. A light intermittent rain fell all morning until one hour before the funeral.

The small log church had people from all around converge upon it. They came from as far as thirty-five miles away. They came in wagons, buggies, two wheel oxcarts, and a few walked and some came on the down train. The church was packed with family members and those who came to pay their last respects and bid her farewell. Small children were quiet as they remained close to their mothers and stared at the strange faces in the church.

Elder Abraham Jackson gave the closing remarks at the funeral as he read from the Ninetieth Psalm of the Old Testament. Afterwards he closed his Bible and wiped a tear from each eye; then composed himself and spoke these words. "When the last trumpet of God shall sound He shall summon her to rise from the Black clay of Ethiopia from which she was created. She shall rise from that hallowed ground and we shall weep no more for her. She will be changed in the blink of an eye from mortality to immortality." Afterwards he sat down and waited for the benediction and the theologians were the first to leave the church building. The wooden casket was loaded on the back of the funeral wagon and taken one hundred yards away to the cemetery. There she was given the last rites and laid to rest.

Chapter Thirty-One

Two months after Nellie's death a horrifying and hideous act which choked the life from the bodies of two African American turpentine workers took place in Statesboro, Georgia. The two men, Paul Reed and Will Cato were lynched and burned alive on a withering August day. Racial disorder and lawlessness in Bulloch County, Georgia attracted people from far and near to this Southeastern rural county, including the counties of Bryan, Emanuel, Laurens, Screven and Tattnall County. Over two hundred men rode the train from Tattnall to Statesboro. Train loads of People converged on the small rural agricultural town of Statesboro. Extra cars had to be added to provide ample transportation for those who came to witness this racial spectacle and miscarriage of justice.

Abraham and his two sons George and Lewis had just returned from Swainsboro on the Wadley Southern and were unaware of the racial terror that occurred in Bulloch County. Elder Jackson and his fellow church members in the county weren't aware of what transpired that day in Bulloch County. The lynching of African American men was nothing new to the people of Georgia and the South. During this tragic period in Georgia's history the lynching of African Americans occurred frequently in every Georgia town large and small. The burning of Black bodies wasn't unfamiliar to any black man, woman, or child living in the county or state. In order to avoid contact with angry individuals or groups, Abraham and his two sons left early in the morning. The three men were armed and well prepared in case they were attacked or fell victim to an angry mob.

They arrived home an hour before dark. Their church meeting lasted around two hours. The train ride was a strenuous task as they stopped in several small towns before arriving at their final destination. The journey was made in part to help mitigate the grief and despair George faced since the death of his wife. The August heat was intense and this made travel on the wood burning train difficult.

Bill knew what time the train arrived and wanted to pick up his father and two brothers at the crossing where it stopped. Their residence was only two hundred yards away. Abraham had Millard and William to care for his prize animal when he traveled long distances. The trip home for the three men was within walking distance from the train. George often joked that he could run the two hundred yards from his house. When Abraham returned home it was a welcome sight as he went to check on his horse Skipper. All of his children were grown and away except the two youngest ones, William and Millard.

Five months later, in January 1905 people were still talking about the horrific murders and the burning of the two African American turpentine workers in the Bulloch County. After church service one Sunday afternoon there was considerable talk of problems in the state associated with the hanging and burning of African Americans. Elders Jackson, Smith, and Williams listened to horror stories of the burning of the bodies of Will Cato and Paul Reed.

"How could a Gawd in heaven allow dis to happen to those poor colored men. Have mercy Lord, on those poor folks family." As Rilla expressed pity for the deceased men.

"Things will get better chilun.' It ain't de end of de world. A lot of colored folks is leaving and going north. Old man Sam Johnson done run away and give up his land." Macy said.

"They kilt Mr. McBride that same night they burned up them poor turpentine workers. They dragged him from his house into the woods. This was one Saturday night and they shot him dead. About ten Ku Klux Klansmen dragged him into the woods, whipped him and shot him. It was awful. Lawd, I hate to think about it; it was sad." Mrs. McCray sobbed, holding back the tears.

"Yes, child, I remember last year, it was awful. Right in the town of Portal where I live; those two turpentine workers were burned up. They broke them out of jail; drug them out of town, poured gasoline on them and burned them up. It was terrible, Lord God it was an awful time." She remembered the fear and the uncontrollable mob riding up to her door that night.

Abraham and the other ministers of the gospel sat and listened as the women spoke about the tragic times in the lives of African American men in the adjoining county of Bulloch. The Black Ministers in Tattnall were concerned for the safety of the members of their race. The group feared for the safety of the African American men, women, and children in their county. They pleaded especially for the young men, to stay away from areas that could cause racial unrest and altercations among the two races. Abraham made known to the ministers in his group and church association that race relations were stable in his close knit community. But it was always best to remain vigilant and work together toward a peaceful solution between the two disparate races. He recognized that a lack of unity among the members of the colored people in his county was a future challenge that needed to be addressed.

"We don't have too many problems with the white people." Elder Smith exclaimed. "It's those new politicians with these new ideas. Tom Watson, he talked about Colored and White farmers having an alliance for their mutual benefit. Later, he tried to turn Colored and White farmers against each other"

"Governor Terrell isn't making things better either. He wants to drive all the Colored people from the state. He said they'd work to run all the niggers out of the Georgia law making body. As soon as that happens, Colored people won't have a chance." Abraham offered his reflection on the problem.

To be located in a small isolated community, Elder Jackson's church increased its membership and the people enjoyed the scenic view. Isolated in terms of distance from other towns, but the people were a close knit group. Abraham continued working hard on his three hundred acre farm. His horse "Skipper" was growing old and he had to limit his pulling of the buggy and wagon for distances of more than ten miles. He purchased a new horse. He had the same striking features as "Skipper." He was a red blaze-faced horse with four white stocking feet. He had the same identical trot and gallop as "Skipper". Bill and Millard claimed that Tom was the ghost of "Skipper."

The following week near the end of January the morning was cool and peaceful. A small sporadic rainfall had fallen most of the night until about an hour before dawn. An hour after daybreak the rain trickled off and stopped completely. The crowing of Abraham's favorite rooster signaled the break of day. After the rain stopped and the weather cleared, he drove his favorite horse "Tom" to the post office three miles away. He was excited and jubilant as he arrived at the post office. He walked over to where the postal worker stood and began a conversation with him smiling. Abraham knew something was happening; he had an inner feeling of ecstasy and excitement.

"How long ago was it preacher that you applied for a pension?" Abraham wanted to hear good news as the man continued talking. "I first saw you back in 1893 or was it 1894? Well preacher, I have good news for you, I think. Here's a letter for you from the Bureau of Pensions."

Abraham was gratified to receive the mail he'd waited for years to receive. He skipped to the buggy where his new horse, "Little Tom" waited for him. As he climbed aboard his buggy, Luke, his friend strolled over to where he was. Luke himself was in high spirits as he spoke to Abraham.

"You sho' looks like someone important today, Elder Jackson."

"Why do you say that Luke; I am the same person that I was yesterday. I'm just a little older. I am almost seventy. And my hair is a little grayer than it was yesterday."

"You know wid your big fine horse and your buggy. You looks like one of them big white farmers. Don't many Colored people have a fine horse; I don't know but one Colored person and he's Sim Padgett."

Abraham was still in a cheerful mood as he arrived at his residence an hour later. Little Tom knew the route of travel he had to take to get to his owner's residence. Bill and Millard were repairing a fence that a wind had blown down three days earlier. They stopped work long enough to place the wagon in the right place and unhitch "Tom" and place him in his stall. They did the same thing with his horse "Skipper" before he became too old to work.

Abraham was glad to see Rilla when he returned home. He looked around to see if Harriet was there. He jokingly told her that she must have an extra room. Because every time he returns home she is there. He strolled to the house smiling. Rilla knew that something strange was going on. She hadn't seen her husband this happy since he first opened his new church.

"Why is you smiling Elder Jackson?" Rilla said, looking at the letter he held in his right hand. "Today ain't your birthday. And you haven't heard from little Abraham, Nancy, or Amanda.

"One more guess, Is Bill getting married?"

"No. I got my first pension check today.

"How much did you get?"

"I'll get ten dollars every month. That's the same amount I got when I was with the Thirty-Third. And that was forty years ago." Abraham said as he saluted a make believe soldier.

"Ten dollars per month is a lot of money, Elder Jackson." Rilla said trying to conceal her excitement.

"Yes, Rilla I prayed hard for this day to come. And ten years later it is here. This is the day of Jubilee"

In the midst of bitter racial strife and despicable attitudes toward African Americans in the county Abraham's Caucasian friends remained loyal to him. They supported him in the work of his church ministry and in his activities outside of the church. His friends signed affidavits for him attesting to his moral soundness as a person and to his integrity as an invalid soldier. Some of the whites in the community ridiculed him as having the support of the scalawags. But they were few in number. His friend Andy was flabbergasted at the white support he received in the county. Andy Holloway was a friend of both Elder Jackson and George. Andy and George owned seventeen lots of land in the new town of Collins.

"Elder Jackson, the hand of God must be upon you. I'm not shocked, but I am dumbfounded at the support you have. You had the support of about as many white folks as Colored folks speak on your behalf. I talked to Jack and Gene and they both said they were friends of the Colored people and always have been."

"Well Andy, when you have the support of both Colored people and White people in the county that make things easier for and old country farmer and country preacher." Abraham divulged.

Elder Jackson and Andy envisioned things were better for African Americans in the Northern part of the county. The two held simultaneous opinions that the problem of racial disharmony and attitudes toward the African American needed to improve in the county as well as statewide. Far too many African American farmers had lost their land through trickery, fraud, and deceit. Other farmers had lost their land through physical and economic intimidation. One of the greatest impediments of the African American farmer was his illiterate condition. This both Elder Jackson and Andy agreed, this made the Colored farmer easy prey for unscrupulous white men in the county. A few Colored men lacked the moral backbone to stand firm and fight to keep their farms.

Chapter Thirty-Two

The New Year 1907 began with a bang. Excitement was in the air; they sang spiritual songs and praised the Lord for the blessings he'd granted to the people in this small community. Abraham's children and grandchildren met at the church to commemorate the forty-fourth anniversary of the signing of the Emancipation proclamation. It was a joyous occasion marked by songs, prayers, and speeches by school children and adults. The children wrote short essays and poems acknowledging President Lincoln for bringing freedom to their grandparents and older relatives. The observance of Emancipation Day lasted four hours. This was the largest sanctification of the celebration since January 1863.

Five months later Sim Padgett and his family became the latest victims of racial hatred in the state since the brutal murders of Paul Reed and Will Cato in the summer of 1904. The afternoon was quiet and peaceful as Mr. Padgett and his family climbed into his surrey buggy to take a trip to the county seat. Three miles before entering Reidsville they were surprised by a group of armed men on horseback with rifles. Sim Padgett had migrated iinto Georgia from South Carolina. He purchased two hundred seventy-five acres of land and cleared the land for farming. He was attacked and his entire family was killed except for one young man who barely escaped.

The lingering thought of the racial atrocities inflicted upon African American men in Portal and Statesboro, Georgia were fresh in the minds of African Americans in Tattnall County. Sebastian "Bootus" McBride was shot and killed after defending his wife from a lynch mob who attacked and whipped her three days after she gave birth. The lynching of Albert Rogers in Statesboro on August 17, 1904 and his son and the shooting death of Handy Bell continued to inflame the fires of racial hatred throughout Southeast, Georgia.

Tension ran high in the county after the Padgett family was lynched and murdered. African American families in the county stayed close to their homes and in their communities. The talk of Klan activity and the whipping and intimidation of African Americans alerted General and Lewis to be vigilant against mob violence. They were warned by Abraham and George not to travel outside the community after dark. Their White friends continued to support Abraham and his family in the midst of the lingering racial turmoil.

A week later General, Lewis, and seventy-two year old Aberdeen were cutting logs as a tree fell, just missing General's head. A limb knocked his hat off knocking him to the ground. They had paused for a second as Aberdeen cautioned them as to what he'd do if caught by a lynch mob. The African American people in the entire community were visibly shaken from the racial horror that happened in Bulloch County. During a break from the hard task of felling trees Aberdeen visibly demonstrated how he was going to protect himself.

"I heard there is going to be a hanging in this county tonight."

"Mr. Aberdeen: Where did you hear that?"

"I heard your Uncle Frank say it General. He heard some white folk talking yesterday."

"Don't worry boys." General snapped. "I have two rabbit foots here; both made of iron." He said pointing toward his two forty-five pistols. "Don't you boys worry; there will be no hanging of Colored people in Tattnall County or Jackson Town tonight."

Later that evening Abraham was engaged in a conversation with his daughter Macy Ann. She was visibly shaken from the fear and idle talk that had invaded the community. She listened intently as Abraham and his son-in-law Abraham Tillman, Tina's husband who assured her everything would be fine in Jackson Town.

"Father Abraham they can hide their faces, but they can't hide the evil that's in their heart. They have been whipping up and hanging poor colored people for years. The buckra have been stealing and taking Colored folk land for years," Mr. Tillman commented.

"That's true. But they don't know all this land belongs to the good Lord. The Bible tells us, that the earth is the Lord's and the people in it. Every since Colored people been in this country they have paid a price that no other race has." Abraham expressed.

"Papa, I don't understand it. You is a preacher and you knows what I mean. What are the Colored people going to do?"

"We must pray; and pray every day and night for this violence to stop."

As the year came to a close the personal property of Sim Padgett was being auctioned off to people who placed their bids for the possessions and goods of the deceased African American farmer. One of the people who attended the auction talked to Elder Jackson three days after he'd left the auction. John Ealey talked to Elder Abraham as he called him about what he'd seen and heard. He participated in the buying of personal property.

"I seed what they did Elder Jackson. I was there."

"What did he have that everyone wanted? I knew he was a good liver."

"Elder Jackson, he had a lot of things. I didn't know a Colored man had that much property. He had school books, a sausage mill, piano, dining table, a two horse wagon, and he had so many things. He had a surrey buggy, two fine mules, and a big red horse like your horse. Jacob was there like I was. He said to me that Sim had well over two hundred acres of land."

"Yes John, the Colored man has fewer and fewer acres of land each year. The Colored man owns just half of the land he had just ten years ago."

Abraham thought of the contradiction between the human rights of man, and the inhumane treatment inflicted upon the Colored people in the state of Georgia. The lynching of these African American men portrayed the darkest days in the nation's history. It was the triumph of evil over good and the decisive rule of barbarism over civility. Abraham said to his congregation two weeks after the chaotic breakdown of law and order in Statesboro and Reidsville; lynching is a crime against law-abiding Caucasian and African American people; and a reproach to a republican form of government.

Elder Jackson's thoughts took him back to the days of slavery in the South. He reflected on the fifty lashes he received for not changing his name from Abraham Jackson to Abraham Collins. He meditated on the time when he emphatically exploded and declared that no white people were going to heaven. He cogitated on Christians and the Christian Church and how the followers of Jesus sanctioned the savage and uncivilized act of burning human beings alive. In a meeting with Elders Lanier and Smith shortly after the tragic deaths of the Padgett family he dramatically asserted that Christian brotherhood was based upon love; not the color of a man's skin. He hammered this point across to them as they sat quietly and hearkened to his every word. If this was untrue, he declared, Christianity was both a hoax and a travesty.

Elder Jackson frequently meditated on the issue of race relations. He believed that the twentieth century would bring with it hope and change. He wrestled with the thought, whether White and colored men served the same God. And at times he questioned his own character and belief.

Chapter Thirty-Three

It was the spring of 1908; a year had nearly passed since the tragic killing of the Padgett family. George was remarried in 1907 to a young woman he'd met three years earlier. It was rumored that he remarried too early after his wife's death. He needed someone to help raise his four young children. They were both attracted to each other and decided to marry through mutual agreement. Her name was Viola Brewton and she was thirty-one years of age, tall and attractive. Her new stepchildren thought she wasn't as pretty as their mother and had a difficult time accepting her. George and Nellie's two oldest children showed more displeasure in the acceptance of their new mother than the five younger children. Viola treated all of her stepchildren with love and care.

Three months later, in the summer of 1908 Ida was married to Jeremiah Bacon. The two were married by Elder Jackson Ida's grandfather. Ida whose nickname was "Sis" was twenty years of age and George and Nellie's oldest daughter. In 1904 she was sixteen and George reminded her she had to help care for her new born brother and the other younger children. She accepted this responsibility with delight and self-assurance. She was especially fond of her four year old brother little James and her nine year old sister Ethel. After her marriage to Jeremiah Ida and Jeremiah moved into one of her father's one room tenant houses' on his three hundred acre farm.

Early the next day Willie came to George's to tell him the latest news he'd heard.

"Mr. George, I heard the Klan is gwine to march tomorrow." Willie nervously said, rubbing his forehead. "Show is hot today, ain't it Mr. George.

"Who told you that Willie?" George asked.

"A white man told me Mr. George."

"Why would the Klan have a march in Reidsville tomorrow? I don't understand Willie."

"I'll be there Bud with old Betsy." General grinned. It'll give me a chance to pull off their white sheets and masks." George and General rode off in the wagon. General's tall body towered high above George as they drove off. "The Padgett family has been dead about a year, and nothing has been done about it."

George rode off about fifty yards and abruptly stopped and climbed down from the wagon. "He had a lot of land, he and his wife and children cleared the land themselves. He had lots of hogs and cows." George had known Sim since he came into the county from South Carolina.

"That ain't no reason to kill a man and his family," General echoed.

George wanted to hurry back home. He climbed back into the wagon and was ready to move on as General motioned for him to stop. "Bud let me catch a ride with you back to Lewis' place. I've got to talk to papa tomorrow as well. I've got to check with Bill too." Both General and George rode away in the wagon en route to their father's house.

The next day General went to the small town to see if Bill was there. As he entered the store he heard the storekeeper talking to Bill about his age.

"How old are you Bill?" He asked.

"I don't know exactly how old I am. Papa said I was born the same year in which the fire broke out in old Fox Bay."

"Bill that was in 1878 or 1879, somewhere back then. Bill you'd either be thirty or twenty-nine. You are Uncle Abram's youngest boy, aren't you?"

"Hey Bud, what are you doing here?" General interrupted.

"I am just talking to Mr. Jim. He thought I was Millard."

"Well General, what can I do for you today? I haven't seen you much. Are you still cutting cross-ties for Morris and the railroad?"

"Let me have five cigars and a soda pop."

"Is that all you want?"

"General, whatever you want I'll get it for you. You can pay me whenever you come this way again."

"I'll see you next Saturday." No one spoke as General left the store. He motioned for Bill to follow him outside.

Later that evening, George, Abraham, and Lewis, were at father's place. They were taking a break from work they were engaged in and began to talk politics; they pondered the problems the Colored people were having in the county and state. Abraham wanted to talk about the problems of disfranchisement and the non-registering of African American voters in Tattnall County. George and Lewis wanted to change the conversation to the lynching of Colored men in the state.

"Why didn't President Roosevelt do something about the lynching of Colored men? Elder Jackson asked. He said colored ministers reflected on the idea of writing President Roosevelt a letter shortly after the lynching of the Padgett family. He even alluded to the fact that they'd talked of petitioning Governor Hoke Smith in the condemnation of the lynching of colored men. Elder Jackson reminded his sons that he talked to the Colored preachers about the killing of Alonzo Williams by a lynch mob in the new county of Toombs in the town of Ohoopee that summer.

"Governor Smith can't be trusted. He is too busy trying to stop Colored men from voting." Andy complained as he walked in. They want people in Georgia to now pay a poll tax. Yes, to pay before you can vote. Something else we will have to do is take a test before we can vote."

"Governor Smith will hurt the buckra too. Lots of them Andy can't read and write. They won't be able to pass no test either. I tell you what Andy, a lot of Colored men is afraid to register to vote."

"Coloreds can't vote in Georgia or in any state in the South. Can they Papa? We done lost our right to vote and ain't nothing we can do." Lewis commented.

"Don't ever think that there isn't anything we can do. One has got to have hope even in things he can't see. That's what we call faith. Last year the last Colored man was kicked out of the Georgia law making body. He was from McIntosh County. Elder Jackson stated."

"Maybe we'll hear from President Roosevelt and Governor Smith. I believe in miracles Elder Jackson. Things is got to change."

Chapter Thirty-Four

Two years later in the summer of 1910 Rilla was growing older and worried about the whereabouts of Nancy and Amanda. She hadn't seen them since 1898; Rilla hadn't seen little Abraham in eighteen years. They had all talked of moving to Savannah since they were old enough to travel on their own. She mentioned to Nellie before she died that Elder Jackson talked so much about the city of Savannah that's why her children left and went there. Rilla still thought that it was possible that she may never see them again. She enjoyed talking and reminiscing with her grandchildren.

"Child, I is getting old now. Your grandpa says I'se blind in one eye and can't see out of the other. Anyway Ida, what is you doing here today? You is married to uh what's his name?"

"His name is Jeremiah grandmamma."

"Mama wants to borrow a cup of sugar. She is going to make a blackberry pie."

"Baby, your old grandmamma have made so many of them blackberry pies. Abram likes them and peas and okra. He used to like a little wine made from them blackberries. But since he started doing the Lord's work, he don't touch nuttin' that looks like wine."

"I thought grandpa liked fried chicken, rice, and tomatoes with sweet potatoes." Ida grinned."

"Here come Abram and his horse "old Tom" and his new buggy. The man he bought his buggy from says if your grandpa takes care of his buggy it'll last him a long time. When he comes in you can ask him, what is his best food?"

"I ain't seen grandpapa in three weeks grandma. Where is he been?"

"He's been so busy him and those other preachers talking about the Colored men that have been hanged. He ain't got time for nothing much."

"Grandma in some of these counties a Colored man is hanged every day; and aint nothing done about it." Ida complained.

The next day the hot summer heat sweltered well above the century mark. Buzzards circled high above the tall pines against a clear blue sky. George and General felt a swoop of cool air upon their head then warm air sweep against their face.

"Steady Bud," George said in a low voice. "We've got to finish this fence today. It's getting hotter and soon we'll have to return to the barn. You've got some work to do and so have I. But I promised papa that we'd finish this fence row."

"This is a bad omen, papa called it a token that is, when something is about to happen and you can't place your finger on it. You know its gwine to happen because you can feel it." General was uneasy as he wiped the sweat from his forehead and gazed up into the clear blue sky. The vultures now flew at a lower altitude than before encircling the area.

"Bud, I remember something like this happened ten years ago. I was on the train when it stopped near Danton. I looked out the train I looked out of the window up into the sky—I saw a swarm of buzzards flying just above the train. Nothing was dead Bud." General exclaimed as he rubbed a trickle of sweat from above his right eye.

"It's a warning, that's what mama called it. That's what it is; when strange things happen we can't explain" General affirmed."

"You are right Bud; it's a warning or a sign that something ain't right. I remember papa telling us something like this happened the same year he kilt that big catamount. A drove of birds flew inside the house against the fireplace. The next day they found a Colored man with his throat cut from ear to ear. No one knew who he was." George said.

"What year was it?"

"It was in 1888 the same year Sis was born. You were fourteen; Bill was ten and Millard was eight.

A week later, General was up early, he'd just eaten breakfast and hitched a team of mules to his large wagon. An hour later a slow drizzle of rain began to fall. As the rain came down the temperature dropped the morning air became cooler. He was dressed in his black boots; wore blue denim breeches and a long sleeve blue shirt. And he wore a large wide brim black hat.

Two of his children peeped outside the door as he hid his forty-five inside his pants pocket. Next he placed his thirty-thirty rifle under his wagon seat. General recalled what'd happen to the Padgett family three years earlier and he didn't want to be surprised by lynching mob. The small drizzle continued to fall barely enough to moisten the grass. Israel had cautioned both George and General the day after they told him of the strange happening they experienced. General was happy and on his way to pick up a roll of wire. He sang as the slow drizzle of rain stopped.

He was a quiet man and didn't bother anyone. He was a giant of a man at six feet and six inches tall and weighed two hundred sixty-five pounds. He was married and had five small children and one grown son. Before 1900 he spent most of his time in the woods cutting timber and cross-ties for the railroad. He enjoyed running the river and rafting timber. He purchased fifteen acres of land from his father. In 1899 as soon as he cleared the land for cultivation he made five bales of cotton on seven acres of land.

General arrived in the small town an hour after he started. He drove his wagon to a hitching post and hitched his two mules and went into the store to purchas a roll of wire that was waiting for him. After he placed his roll of wire in the wagon he stood on the outside of the store and drank a soda pop. Five minutes later, three white men came and stood by where General sat quietly drinking his soda and enjoying the cool air. One of the three men spoke to General in a derogatory manner to denigrate him.

"Gosh darn it, boy you is a tall nigger. How tall is you nigger?" The short rotund man asked trying to provoke a fight with General. He ignored the man. He didn't say a word; General continued to drink his soda.

"Hey boy, preacher I'm talking to you." A second man yelled out, as he raised his voice. "Can you hear nigger? He spoke in an angry voice as he moved a step closer to General.

The rain had stopped and the sun began to shine against an overcast sky. "You talking to me boy; General stared at the man as he spoke in a low key voice. "I am a man not a boy. I am not a nigger, I'm a Colored man. I'm not a preacher and I ain't your uncle. I am thirty-six years old, married and have five children." General said as he moved closer to his wagon where he had his thirty-thirty Winchester rifle under the wagon seat.

A small crowd gathered in the background. General walked slowly towards the first man who spoke. He knocked him to the ground in the mud. The small crowd which moved closer towards General scattered. General took cover behind a large tree as bullets began to ring out. Profanity was used on both sides of the street. There was swearing, cursing, and all kinds of vile language being hurled at General and other people.

A shower of bullets repeatedly came from General's forty five and his thirty-thirty. With his Winchester rifle he sprayed bullets all over the upstairs building where his assailants were hiding upstairs. The bullets coming in rapid fire from his rifle set a box of cartridges on fire in one of his attacker's right pocket. It was seven men against one; and for close to an hour ugly racial epithets and obscene language were launched at General.

Two hours later Abraham, George, and Elza rode into town on Abraham's wagon. This time it was Abraham's two horse wagon; with Old Tom and George's young horse pulling the wagon. General was shot in the stomach and the bullet forced its way out of his right side. Three of the seven men that were shooting at General were wounded. Ike preceded Abraham, Elza, and George in his wagon standing up and hollering out on both sides of the street.

"White folks today I came prepared to die. I will wade in blood knee deep if things don't stop. Just like I said I am prepared to die. Is any among you prepared to die?"

"Don't worry Uncle Ike we'll take care of things." The sheriff nervously spoke. He spoke to the small crowd that had gathered to return to where they needed to go; the disturbance was over and they needed to go home.

The road was boggy and slippery; the wagon wheels screeched and skidded as they moved through the mud. Ike had left his wagon and joined Abraham, George, and Elza in their wagon. He held on to his shotgun as the flat bottomed wagon continued to move making a shrill noise moving through the mud. Abraham's rough face and swollen eyes from a lack of sleep matched his rough looking clothes. Not a whisper was heard among the group or the town people. The sheriff's wrinkled face turned pale as he was about to speak to seventy-three year old Abraham Jackson. He turned to see, what was the noise he heard in the wagon.

Seconds later, a Black man turned the corner riding in a green wagon with red wheels. A large white horse pulled the wagon through the mud as the wheels screeched. Abraham turned around quickly to see if he recognized the man in the wagon. "If I have to go, I am prepared to take a lot of you with me." Abraham was shocked as he heard those words echoed. His thoughts wandered back to when his father was killed. The sheriff interrupted:

"Preacher, we have your boy here." We were waiting for you to come take him away."

"We come to get him." Abraham said as he stepped down from the wagon. Elza and Ike stepped down as George remained in the wagon. Ike had his pistol strapped to his waist and his shotgun in his hand.

"He is lucky the bullet entered in his stomach and went out through his back. He's lost a lot of blood, but he'll live. He'll be okay preacher." The deputy said to Elder Jackson.

"We don't want any trouble white folks. We just came to take him back home; there's been enough blood spilled for one day."

The unidentified man was Lewis who joined the others near where General lay. Lewis laid his rifle against the tree near the hitching post. "Let's take him to Dr. Harris," Lewis said.

"No. Let's take him to cousin's Mariah's around the corner. Dr. Harris can come around to Mariah's house to see him."

"Boys what took you so long to get here? "Don't worry, I'll be alright. I'm as tough as a grizzie bear." General grimaced as he tried to laugh. "Where is Bud?"

"Right here Genera!." George said, as he leaped from the wagon onto the muddy ground. "Hold on, I'm here grizzie." He shouted in a burst of excitement and laughter.

"Let's move out of here" cried Lewis.

Three months later the weekend of the second Saturday and Sunday Elder Jackson and his church held a two day meeting for their Association of Churches. Saturday and Sunday in October 1910 people met in a great assemblage at Jackson Town to have church service. They came from as far away as Savannah to the East and Macon to the West. They came in large numbers, men and women, the young and the aged; both African Americans and Caucasian. Many from the small surroundings communities walked, while others came in wagons, buggies, and some in two wheeled oxcarts. A few Caucasians worshippers had African American buggy drivers. After church service was over tables were set fifty yards long with an overabundance of food to accommodate the large crowds of people. All kinds of food were prepared for the two-day meeting. The people had all kinds of meats; chicken fish, and beef; they also had beans, cabbage, sweet potatoes, and rice. They had lemonade, tea, and water prepared for the people to drink and for dessert all kinds of pies and cakes.

Close to three hundred people were in attendance for the two day meeting. A large brush arbor was built because the small church wasn't constructed to accommodate such a large group of people. A brush arbor was built by George, Lewis, Elza, and Israel. There were seats on both sides and a center aisle for people to walk down. Elder Jackson and his son George had many Caucasian friends who came just to eat and enjoy their fellowship. The church sat on Abraham's three hundred acre tract of land.

It was a mild October day that Saturday. Among the ministers of the gospel who were present that day Were Elder Munlin of Bulloch County and two other African American ministers; two White ministers of the gospel, Elder Sanders and Elder Carswell. And from the local churches in the area were Elders Lanier, Robinson, Williams, and Elder Jackson and Elder Bill Robinson from Beth Haven.

Chapter Thirty-Five

It was the last month of the year in 1911. Abraham was notified by county officials that a new road would be built that would run through a narrow strip of his property. The new road would intersect the Cobb Town and Reidsville Road leading to the corner of George Jackson's fence marker. George had already given a portion of his land to construct the Wadley Southern Railroad back in the 1890s. Abraham and George didn't protest the building of the new road. They were happy to see a road that would provide smooth travel for them to their residence.

Abraham turned seventy-four in May and didn't travel as much as he once did. George and Lewis traveled to the courthouse for their father. Rilla was sixty-eight and had just suffered a stroke in November. She had grown weaker, but still had the use of her hands and feet. She didn't stand for long periods of time, but enjoyed sitting and telling her grandchildren stories. She was fond of telling them stories after she finished her work. Rilla had the children to come around her bed which was more comfortable. Each of her grandchildren took turns looking after her well-being. Her left leg and foot were immobile and she walked with the aid of a walking stick.

Rilla's stories left the children spellbound. "Let me tell you chilun' 'bout where old Massa Collins and Miss Sarah lived; If you were in the area you'd break your neck getting out 'before dark. I heard they were a short man that walked around with no head on his body.'

"Did you ever see him grandma?" Hattie and Ethel asked in a squeaky voice.

"I didn't ever see anything, but I heard things. I heard doors open and shut. And late at night I heard pots and pans fall to the floor. Lawd, your grandpa used to get after me. He said I was scared of my shadow. When he was in Abe Lincoln's army, Macy Ann and Harriet were scared. But George, Lewis, and Tina, nothing scared them. I heard Abe Lincoln's soldiers were scared to come in this area."

"That was a long time ago grandma. I ain't scared. Is you scared Hattie?" Ethel grinned.

"Yes, that was close to fifty years ago. Chilun' you'd better go from around my bed. Abram will be home soon. He don't believe what I tell you is true. But he has heard and seen some things."

"Tell us grandma, what did grandpapa hear and see?" Utah asked.

"I'll tell you tomorrow." Rilla said.

Later the next day when it was warmer George and Lewis went to the courthouse to find out more about the new road that was to pass through Abraham's land stop at George's fence corner. While there Lewis overheard a conversation between two men about their land.

"I want that nigger Abraham's land Floyd. And you are going to help me get it. I don't know Joe, he is one of them crazy niggers."

"What do you mean Floyd? None of them niggers can read and write. How do you think we got that Eason nigger's farm? A lot of them just left their farms and didn't pay the taxes on the land."

Lewis had his head down and pretended he didn't hear anything. The men kept talking as Lewis listened carefully. George had to check to see if he'd paid all of his taxes. Lewis reflected to himself that in 1899 they tried to take his land for nonpayment of taxes.

"Floyd, just check the tax office and see if Uncle Abe and Uncle George paid their taxes. Check the years 1908 and 1909; that should tell us something. If we ain't careful those niggers will own all the land around here."

"I'm going to talk to the sheriff and see if he has anything. If we ain't careful the niggers will be trying to marry our women next" Joe grinned.

Three years later in 1914 the county made an effort to undergo change that would bring it in step with present day modernization. Two new counties were created from Tattnall; Evans and Candler counties. Parts of Toombs County were created from Tattnall in 1905. But in matters of race the county continued on a path to maintain the status quo. Politicians continued to publicly appeal to white voters through newspaper advertisements. The convict lease system continued the practice of using an overwhelming number of African Americans to work on county roads and farms. An overwhelming majority of the former slaves were unable to read and write.

The last week in February a heavy snow fell in Jackson Town and Collins. The largest snow in the area in fifteen years fell in the county that night. That same day, a tragedy happened to Macy Ann and Israel's oldest son Jesse. He was shot to death in the newly created county of Toombs in Lyons, Georgia that Saturday afternoon. He was shot to death by a white man who claimed Jesse's girlfriend was his woman. "Jesse's friend said, the white man pulled out his pistol and shot poor Jessie. The man then called him a nigger and started cussing him as he lay dying."

The next afternoon Macy Ann and Israel were at Abraham and Rilla's house grieving over their son's death. Millard not knowing what had happened spoke to Macy Ann and Israel.

"Hello sis, hello Israel, how are you two doing this afternoon. How did you get through all of that snow? I ain't never seen so much snow." Millard continued to talk. He surmised something was wrong by the look on their faces. "What's wrong sis, you two look like you just came from a funeral."

"I'll tell him Macy."

"Tell me what." Millard cried out.

"No. I'll tell him," Abraham interrupted. "Jesse is dead Babe. He was shot up in Lyons last night by a white man. He was shot about a colored woman."

"Macy Ann wept as she talked. "That man is gwine to burn in hell. Hear me mama and papa. They is gwine to be placed in hell; all who had something to do with my son's death. I'll be right there in hell to make sure he burns. I'll start the fire myself, to make sure it burns." Macy Ann cried out.

Abraham walked over and placed his arms around Macy to console her. He said he felt the pain she felt; and the hurt she experienced. He'd seen far too much violence and death inflicted upon African American men and women. "We are all of God's children; the Colored people and the White People. He made us all in his image. Child, I know it's hard, but don't you become full of hate like them. Did you hear me Mace you and Israel? Yes child, God will take care of everything." Abraham admonished.

It was Christmas Eve and singing and laughter could be heard a mile away from George's house. The air outside was cold as the temperature was just a few degrees above freezing. Abraham's buggy with Old Tom pulling it moved closer to George's house. Suddenly, the singing and laughter ceased as he arrived at George's residence.

Bill and Millard had been with George all morning; Harriet, Mace, and Israel were present. Lewis arrived thirty minutes before Abraham. Rilla was gravely ill and unable to come. She suffered a debilitating stroke in 1912 and was confined to a wheelchair. She had ten of her grandchildren there to help take care of her. The younger ones rotated their duty in caring for her. She was upbeat and jolly each day; always telling the grandchildren stories to keep them happy and laughing.

It was a big day for Ethel, George and Nellie's youngest daughter. Today she was getting married to William; a man she met six months earlier at Bethaven Church. A well-dressed and neatly groomed man whom George had given permission to see his youngest daughter. The singing and laughter continued. Harriet and Bill were engaged in acts of humor. The entire family that was present were animated and exuberant. It was a joyous occasion; George and Nellie's youngest daughter were getting married. Millard reminded Lewis that they hadn't had that much fun since Ida's wedding in 1908.

Abraham arrived in his buggy and George was thrilled to see him as Millard tied Tom to the hitching post. "Hello papa," George grinned as Elder Jackson climbed from the buggy. "Hurry up papa and let's go inside. It's too cold for you to be standing around. Millard take care of Tom for papa."

"I ain't as young as I used to be. My old bones are getting stiff now."

George and Viola had a large fire burning in the fireplace. A heater was on the other side of the large living room. All of the smaller children were in one room. It was cold outside but viola was cooking in the kitchen. She was cooking cakes and pies she'd made especially for the wedding. She had a long table in the center of the dining room that could seat twelve people. Her cakes and pies were placed in the middle of the table. George had his best blackberry wine that he'd prepared just for this occasion.

Abraham was dressed for the occasion. He wore his navy blue suit and had on his white shirt with ruffles; and his goatee beard was neatly trimmed. He appeared to be the twin brother of Frederick Douglas. "Papa I'm glad you're on time; you were late for Jeremiah and Sis's wedding six years ago in 1908. Papa, did anyone ever mistaken you to be the twin brother of Frederick Douglass."

"Papa, how is mama doing? I didn't get a chance to see her yesterday."

"She's doing fairly well. You know your children and Lewis' children are there most of the time. Bill's children are there a lot. She doesn't get lonely for company." Abraham beamed.

"Let's hurry and finish everything. I am hungry and thirsty and ready to eat." Bill grinned. I've got to get back home before it freezes. My old mule, Daisy is real slow when it's cold."

"She ain't that fast when it's warm either. We is gwine to stay with mama and papa tonight. Papa already told us to come by. Didn't he Charles?" Harriet said.

"Remember William Jackson, this ain't your wedding. You were married six years ago. After your wedding, papa had to run you out of that hotel. Don't you drink too much blackberry wine either." Harriet looked at Macy and chuckled.

"Anyway Bill you is too old to jump over a broom. You may fall down and hurt yourself." George laughed.

Elder Jackson performed the wedding ceremony at 3:30 in the afternoon. George and Nellie's third youngest daughter was married to William Nash. Many people not related to Abraham would always ask him about his service in the union army. His favorite saying to everyone who asked was "I'm not a soldier anymore. My job now is working for the good Lord until he calls me home."

Three months later, on March 12, 1915 Rilla suffered a massive stroke and was confined to the bed; she died three days later on March 15, 1915 with her children by her bedside. Abraham broke down and wept when he learned of her death. She'd been there for him each and every day since the end of slavery. He remembered that she was the one who could've saved his life during the time he was brutally and severely beaten. The thoughts of her continually bombarded his mind. The family sent for Dr. Harris to examine her two hours after she passed.

A month later in April 1915 Abraham said to Bill "at this point in my life, time is my only enemy Bill. He set up and looked around. "I am too old to run away. Anyway the Massa's old dog would tear me apart." Abraham growled. "Where is George?" Bill walked outside to get George. George hurriedly walked inside to see what had taken place.

"Papa is talking out of his head" Bill made known to George.

"Papa, what are you talking about? You are too old to run away and dogs chasing after you and tearing you apart." George wanted to know what was going on.

"At my door death knocks, but I will not answer. In death one lies quiet and still." Abraham spoke in a quiet hoarse voice. "But with life flowing through your body you are strong and vibrant; ready to answer any call." George had never heard his father speak like this. George and Bill were shocked at the words spoken by their father.

Ethel whom he married in December came around to see her grandfather and find out how he was doing. He talked to her about the schoolhouse. "Ethel, you'll teach at that school one day." He grinned.

"I am too young grandpa. I don't know anything about teaching." Ida is teaching up there. Try not to talk too much grandpa . . ." Ethel sent for her papa George to come into the room.

Outside it was a cold windy day as Abraham lay quiet and motionless in bed. Seconds later he began to talk incoherently as if he heard voices. "Where is Babe? I saw him ten minutes ago; he needs to put some wood on the fire. Come here Bill you and Babe. Abraham continued to cry out for the two of them. An hour later, Abraham died of pneumonia at the age of seventy-eight. He was buried a week later in the cemetery that was named for him."